Live, Listen, Tell

The Art of Preaching

Geoff New

Langham
PREACHING RESOURCES

© 2017 by Geoff New

Published 2017 by Langham Preaching Resources
an imprint of Langham Creative Projects

Langham Partnership
PO Box 296, Carlisle, Cumbria CA3 9WZ, UK
www.langham.org

ISBNs:
978-1-78368-162-4 Print
978-1-78368-164-8 Mobi
978-1-78368-163-1 ePub
978-1-78368-165-5 PDF

Geoff New has asserted his right under the Copyright, Designs and Patents Act, 1988 to be
identified as the Author of this work.

All Scripture quotations, unless otherwise indicated, are taken from the Holy Bible, New
International Version®, Anglicised, NIV®. Copyright © 1979, 1984, 2011 by Biblica, Inc.® Used by
permission. All rights reserved worldwide.

British Library Cataloguing in Publication Data
A catalogue record for this book is available from the British Library

ISBN: 978-1-78368-162-4

Cover & Book Design: projectluz.com

This is a book that guides us to live, listen and tell. As we do that we ourselves as well as our listeners will experience hope and light. I have always appreciated the Ignatian Gospel Contemplation as a spirituality exercise but to link it with sermon preparation in such a creative way is Geoff New's genius skill. When I was asked to write an endorsement for a book on preaching I sighed and murmured to myself whether we do really need another book on preaching. Now that I have read the manuscript I have a totally different story to tell. This is a book that deserves listening and telling!

Rev Riad Kassis, PhD
Director, Langham Scholars
International Director, International Council for Evangelical Theological Education

What Geoff New offers in this book is a crucial but oft-neglected step in the process of sermon preparation. Preachers first need to hear God from the text for themselves, something that many homiletic books assume but seldom give guidance on. Geoff New takes you step-by-step from listening to God through *lectio divina* and Ignatian Gospel Contemplation to formulating a sermon outline. This will change your sermon from merely transmitting facts to transforming lives by enabling others to listen to God as well.

Rev Maggie Low, PhD
Old Testament and Homiletics Lecturer
Trinity Theological College, Singapore

Geoff New has given the homiletic world a gift, a new spiritual paradigm, under which preachers can tune in to God's voice with freshness, creativity and transforming power. *Live, Listen, Tell* has brought back beautiful memories of my spiritual exercises with the Jesuits. Thank you, Geoff!

Jorge Atiencia
Langham Preaching, Colombia

Such is the effect of reading this book that I cannot now read my Bible without praying out loud. This book is unique in that it revives a long forgotten art in which believers read their Bible with a heart already surrendering to the Lord who speaks through the Bible in a living and active way throughout all the ages.

Rev Ma'afu Palu, PhD
Head of Department of Biblical Studies
Sia'atoutai Theological College, Tonga

Geoff New's book is not a theological book that is difficult to read. It is instead a manual which gives preachers the joy of knowing "we can do it." Asian immigrants in New Zealand are living in three worlds – the world of their faith/tradition from Asia, the world of being immigrants in New Zealand, and the world of interculturalism. Honestly, it is a big burden for Asian preachers to prepare a sermon which is appropriately related to the three worlds of their church members.

Live, Listen, Tell will be a big help because Geoff suggests practical guidelines of "living a story, listening to a story and telling a story" which will lighten the burden of preachers from Asia and around the world. The Bible is full of stories of immigrants who live, listen and tell. Geoff reminds us that the essential skills of a preacher are to "Read the Bible Aloud, Think Deeply, Pray Honestly and Rest Quietly." I strongly believe that this book is a hospitable invitation for settlers and immigrants to live a story, listen to a story and tell a story together. Let us accept it and enjoy having our lives shaped by God.

Rev Kyoung Gyun Han
Asian Ministries Coordinator
Presbyterian Church of Aotearoa, New Zealand

Before you can speak God's word, it has to speak to you. But how do you hear it speak? That is the question Geoff New answers in *Live, Listen, Tell*.

Jennifer Cuthbertson
Coordinator for Trainer Development, Langham Preaching

For Talia

Your art, writing and speaking give people words and vision to see life in new and exciting ways.

CONTENTS

Preface

When I was a teenager I attended an all-boys school. One day in class my English teacher said we were going to study *Romeo and Juliet*. I could not believe it. He was going to teach a love story to a class of sixteen-year-old boys? I remember thinking that this was going to be terrible and that I would be totally bored. I could not have been more wrong.

That year of studying *Romeo and Juliet* changed my life. I know that is a big claim but it is true. The reason why studying a 400-year-old romance was so powerful was because of my teacher. He did not simply teach English as a subject; he loved it. Teaching English was a lifestyle, not a job. As he taught the class about *Romeo and Juliet* he explained what the ancient words, poetry and events meant. The story became alive and exciting. He taught me how to understand an ancient text today. Ever since my first introduction to *Romeo and Juliet*, whenever I discover the story is being performed by a local drama group or if a new movie version is released, I am there. Watching and listening to the story all over again. I love it. My experience of learning the story of *Romeo and Juliet* and how to study it and make sense of it today actually has helped me as a preacher. The skills my English teacher taught me and the way he showed his love of his work inspired me for life. Later, after I became a Christian, God took some of that experience and shaped it so that I could understand and live in the greatest love story of all time: God sending his Son, Jesus Christ, because he loved the world. Now the story that my life is dedicated to is found in the Scriptures, and my time is spent studying them, preaching them and helping people understand them. My life is dedicated to the Author of the greatest story ever. A never-ending story.

And so now to this book you are reading. What has *Romeo and Juliet* got to do with a book about preaching? One day, over thirty years after I first discovered *Romeo and Juliet*, my niece, Talia (thirteen years old at the time), sent me something she had written about the play. She was studying it in her English class. She did not know my love for the story and it was a special moment when I received her work. I am not really sure what happened as I read her retelling of this story, but it proved the means of reflecting in new ways on the importance of preaching the Word of God. God spoke to me through Talia's writing. God does tend to speak in unexpected ways! As I wrote back to her, new thoughts came to my mind about how we live life in relation to our Lord God. I wrote this:

> Your writing is . . . a gift. Your telling of the story is a unique and wonderful telling of the story. It is powerful. You have a rare gift.
>
> The thing about this world is that people are doing three things: living a story (their own), listening to stories (those around them) and telling stories (a mix of the previous two). Their world and the way they are as people are powerfully formed by these three kinds of stories: living, listening and telling.
>
> The thing the world most needs are people who can do all three well. There aren't that many who can. I suggest you are one of the few who can.

My prayer for you as you read this book is that the Spirit of God will empower and inspire you to live, listen and tell the story of Jesus Christ in ways which change you and continue to change the world. My prayer for you is that your love for the Scriptures will deepen and widen, and that your love for the Author of Life will abound.

> Now to him who is able to do immeasurably more than all we ask or imagine, according to his power that is at work within us, to him be glory in the church and in Christ Jesus throughout all generations, for ever and ever! Amen. (Eph 3:20–21)

Geoff New
Christmas 2015

1

The Story of Your Life

This is a book *for* preachers *about* preaching. Whether you are the pastor of your church or a member of your church, even if you preach only once a year, if you preach, this book is for you.

You might think because this is a book for preachers and about preaching, it will be about speaking. You might think this is a book about what to say to the people who listen when you preach. Maybe you think this is a book about how to write a sermon; how to study the Bible and prepare the words to preach.

Of course, this book will include those topics. But its focus is on how to listen to God as you study the Scriptures when you are preparing your sermon. When you hear what God wants to say through your sermon, everything changes. The way you preach changes. What you say when you preach changes. The people listening to your sermon change. If you hear and meet with God during your sermon preparation, when you stand before your people, you will be able to say, "I have seen the Lord!" By the end of the sermon, the people will respond, "As have we!" If you know what God is saying to you as a preacher, when you preach you will not just deliver a sermon. You live the sermon!

It is obvious that, as a preacher, you need to understand the Bible. The Bible is what you preach from. But it is not enough for you to only understand the Bible. It is important that you understand who the Bible is for: people. I love how one of the great church leaders from centuries ago, Augustine, described the Bible. He said it is like "a letter from home." The Bible is a letter from God to people. Preachers will often study the Bible, but they will not always study people. A much respected preacher in my country liked to do nothing better on his day off than go and sit in the airport and watch people. He learnt so much from sitting there for hours watching people saying goodbye to each other as they left and others arriving greeting each other with joy. He was such a good preacher because he knew the Bible and he knew people.

It can be tricky understanding people though. Everyone is so different and people have secrets, problems, pain, hope, love and gifts. Yet even though people are all so different, we do share some things in common. One of the things we share is the way our lives grow and are shaped. Think of people's lives as a story. We all have this in common. Our lives are a story. The challenge for preachers is to faithfully tell God's story so that it is the story that we live our stories by. But first, let's consider how people's lives can be understood as a story.

All of us are *living* a story, *listening* to a story and *telling* a story.[1] Often we do not even think about it because the story we live, listen to and tell is what we do from the moment we wake up every day. Our living, listening and telling is what makes up our very life. We all are living lives which are in need of the in-breaking message and Word of Christ. So the starting point is lives which are a mixture of faithfulness and faithlessness to God. The story we live is in constant need of "listening to the story of Christ" so that the "story we tell" changes and therefore the "story we live" changes. Without even trying all of us are *living* a story, *listening* to a story and *telling* a story.

Think about young children. The story they live includes the time and country they are born into. Their parents and family are part of the story they are living. The kind of home they live in is part of the story they are living. All children are living a story long before they are able to walk or talk.

We are living a story.

Slowly babies begin to learn their names and the sound of their parents' voices. Slowly they learn to listen and understand. This begins to change the life they are living. They turn their head at the sound of their mother's voice. They experience happiness and comfort as they listen to loving voices.

We are listening to a story.

In time children begin to learn to speak. Just one word to start with. Maybe it is not even said correctly, but it is beautiful. Then more words are learnt and soon children are telling a story every time they speak.

---

1. In this book I use the order (i) living, (ii) listening and (iii) telling. However, life is never quite that neat and tidy, and so sometimes the order is experienced differently. Imagine a three-strand cord. If we were to label each strand "living," "listening" and "telling," we would see each strand as separate *and* bound together to make one cord. Each strand is individual and also overlapping another, with the order always changing. However, so as to best illustrate the relationship between living/listening/telling, I will describe them as happening in order: (i) living, (ii) listening and (iii) telling.

We are telling a story.

Living a story, listening to a story and telling a story. If you are aware of these three parts of life you will become a better preacher, because you will understand yourself, others and God better. You will see that where people live, how they live, and who they live with is the story they live. You will see that the voices they hear and what those voices say form the story people listen to. You will see this helps create the story people then tell. Let me give you an example.

Nagaland is a state in northeast India. The Nagas are a warm people who love to welcome you into their homes and country. They also love God. Ninety-five percent identify themselves as Christian. I went there to teach pastors and leaders how to preach, and I took a small team from the church in New Zealand I was pastoring. As we travelled from the airport along the roads and into the hills of Nagaland, we noticed something. The hills and plains are wide open, but the houses in the villages are built wall to wall. This is part of the story they live. Why are the houses built so close together? Because of a story the Nagas have listened to about their culture and history. Listen to Visakhonu Hibo (Christian leader, college principal and author) from Nagaland as she tells some of the story:

> Before the gospel came to Nagaland, the Nagas were headhunters who lived in little independent villages isolated from each other. They hunted heads to scare away enemies and sickness. Hunting heads was also a way to earn prestige and honour for their villages. However the main reason headhunting was practised was to keep the women and children safe.

So even though headhunting has not been practised for many, many years, the Nagas still build their houses close together for protection. The houses are so close together that they form a small fortress. The story they have listened to affects the story they live and the story they tell. While headhunting is no longer practised, it still influences the way villages are built. The stories of the past cannot be told without explaining that part of their history. We are all affected by our own stories in the same way. The story we listen to shapes the story we live today and the story we tell.

God's story, the Bible, begins to change the story we are living. You will begin to see that preaching is one of the ways which our Father in heaven speaks to his children.

The stories we *listen* to powerfully shape the story we *live* and the story we *tell*. We live in a fallen world. Genesis 1–2 tells us that this world has been beautifully created by God. Genesis 3 tells us how that beauty has been damaged by sin. Left to ourselves we tend to live, listen to and tell stories which are godless. This means that the story we live has a desperate need for God. One of the very first things the Bible tells us about God is that he spoke (Gen 1:3). When God speaks and people listen, the stories they live and tell change. As a preacher you need to understand this.

So the first skill preachers need is listening. If preachers do not listen to what the Spirit is saying to the church through the Scriptures, then they do not really have anything worth saying when they preach. Listening is the most important skill a preacher needs to learn because your sermon becomes the story people listen to. Your sermon will be the way God changes the story they live and the story they tell.

Think about the stories you listened to as you were growing up. Stories about how your parents met each other. Or maybe stories about the tricks your uncles and aunties played on each other when they were growing up. You might have heard stories about something brave a family member once did. Those stories shape us. Think of the stories about your church. I was the pastor of a church for seventeen years, and that church remembers the story of when it was first planted in 1958. Every year in November we would have a special service of thanksgiving and we remembered that story. We loved it. Once, as a church, we spent time answering the question "Tell us about when, during a worship service here, you were most alive and excited about worship. What happened?" The stories told went back over fifty years. It was powerful. Those kinds of stories shape us. Such stories change us because we gain fresh reminders of the work and presence of God among us. At its best, listening to good stories gives us hope and light. Christianity has been described as a religion of revelation. That means that when we listen to the story of God through the Bible, God's Spirit gives us understanding about a new way of living. We discover we are loved by God and through Jesus Christ we have peace with him. When we listen to God's story and we respond to him, our life is shaped in new ways. The Bible often uses the example of a potter and clay to talk about this kind of thing (Isa 64:8). We are shaped and moulded like clay in the potter's hand. Listening carefully to the story of God in the Scriptures is one of the most important ways our lives are shaped by God.

Living a story, listening to a story and telling a story. Which story do you listen to the most? Which story has the greatest impact on your life? Which story guides your life? If you are a preacher, your answer will probably be something like, "The story of the Bible. The story of how God loves the world, sent his Son to save the world, and sent the Holy Spirit to help us serve God's mission until the return of Christ." Or we might say that as Christians we listen to the Christmas story (God comes in humility), the Easter story (God comes in love) and the Pentecost story (God comes in power).

So, which story do you listen to the most? Test your answer by asking yourself "What story am I living?" and "What story am I telling?" Think about the day-to-day things you do and talk about with others. Do they match the story you say you listen to the most? Is the way you live and are the things you tell others marked by the Christmas, Easter and Pentecost stories? If you want to *really* know which story you *really* listen to, think about your way of life and the way you speak. That will show you most clearly which story you are *really* listening to. Let me give you another example.

Jasmine is a young Christian woman who was very excited about preparing for her wedding. However, less than two weeks before her wedding day, her eighteen-year-old cousin died suddenly. I went to see Jasmine. She was deeply shocked. She told me that she felt selfish about continuing to prepare for her wedding; she wanted to grieve for and honour her cousin.

I paused, because I knew what I wanted to say but was unsure whether she would be able to hear it. I knew the story I wanted to tell but I was unsure whether Jasmine could really hear it in her sadness and grief. But I decided to say it anyway. So I began to talk to Jasmine about the Easter story. I told her that her wedding and her cousin's death were not totally separate events and that, just like in the Easter story, we live with darkness and light, grief and joy. There is no separation. That is, in the Easter story, Jesus in the garden of Gethsemane prays that his own death won't happen. Then the cross happens, for all our sake. And then three days later, we see an empty tomb in a garden because he is victorious and he rose from the dead. Darkness and light, death and life, grief and joy are all part of it. I finished speaking and paused.

She said, "Yes, my fiancé and I talked about that just last night." I did not expect someone so young to respond so thoughtfully. Clearly, she had been listening to the story of Jesus very well. She was living the story, listening to the story and telling the story beautifully. She went to her cousin's funeral and her own wedding in the same week. She and her family all had *listened* to the story very well. How do I know? Because I watched them *live* the story, and I heard them *tell* the story. They lived faith and talked about hope because they had listened to the story of God's love.

The Bible contains wonderful examples of how people *lived* a story, *listened* to a story and *told* a story. Consider the story of the prophet Isaiah as told in Isaiah 6. In the year that King Uzziah dies, Isaiah sees the Lord (the living King) on his throne in the temple (Isa 6:1–4). Isaiah is confronted by the vision of the Lord and confronted with the story he has been living. Isaiah describes that story in these words: "Woe to me! I am ruined! For I am a man of unclean lips, and I live among a people of unclean lips, and my eyes have seen the King, the Lord Almighty" (Isa 6:5). This is the story Isaiah is living.

Then he experiences God's forgiveness (Isa 6:6–7) and hears a new story. "Then I heard the voice of the Lord saying, 'Whom shall I send? And who will go for us?'" This is the story Isaiah is listening to.

"And I said, 'Here am I. Send me!'" (Isa 6: 8). Isaiah is then empowered to tell a story. God says to him, "Go and tell this people . . ." (Isa 6:9). The prophet receives the message from God to preach. This is the story Isaiah tells.

The story Isaiah tells leads us to another example: the Ethiopian eunuch in Acts 8. In Acts 8:26–40, a powerful government official from Ethiopia has been in Jerusalem worshipping at the temple (Acts 8:27). This is the story he was living. Then on his way home he is reading the book of Isaiah but he doesn't understand it. Meanwhile the Spirit has led Philip to the Ethiopian. Philip runs up to the Ethiopian's chariot and asks if he understands what he is reading. The Ethiopian admits that he doesn't and invites Philip onto his chariot. "The eunuch asked Philip, 'Tell me, please, who is the prophet talking about, himself or someone else?' Then Philip began with that very passage of Scripture and told him the good news about Jesus" (Acts 8:34–35). This is the story the Ethiopian listens to. Then Philip baptizes him and the Spirit carries Philip away and the Ethiopian eunuch "went on his way rejoicing" (Acts 8:39). He has a new story to tell. Tradition has it that the Christian church in Ethiopia had its beginnings in this encounter.

Living a story, listening to a story and telling a story. Seeing this pattern in people's lives is important as you preach to them. Let's consider one particular chapter in the Bible which helps us see this pattern. Hebrews 11 lists men and women who lived and told the story of God because they *listened* to his story and believed. Hebrews 11 is a wonderful place to gain strength and inspiration to see how to live, listen and tell the story of God. Preachers need to master all three but they must be best at listening deeply and carefully because only then will they live and tell the story "according to the Scriptures."

The first example in Hebrews 11 is that of Abel (v. 4):

> By faith Abel brought God a better offering than Cain did. By faith he was commended as righteous, when God spoke well of his offerings. And by faith Abel still speaks, even though he is dead.

Do you see the pattern?

- Living the story
  "By faith Abel brought God a better offering than Cain did."

  Abel made an offering to God.

- Listening to the story
  "By faith he was commended as righteous, when God spoke well of his offering."

  Abel listened to God and learnt how to worship him.

- Telling the story
  "And by faith Abel still speaks, even though he is dead."

  Abel's faith and the injustice he suffered is still told.

Let's look at another example, Noah (v. 7):

> By faith Noah, when warned about things not yet seen, in holy fear built an ark to save his family. By his faith he condemned the world and became heir of the righteousness that is in keeping with faith.

- Living the story
  "By faith Noah . . . in holy fear built an ark to save his family."

  Noah builds a boat.

- Listening to the story
  "when warned about things not yet seen"

  Noah hears the Word of God about the coming flood.

- Telling the story
  "By his faith he condemned the world and became heir of the righteousness that is in keeping with faith."

  Noah walked faithfully with God and his obedience exposed the sin of others.

In Hebrews 11, the writer gathers up the stories of these men and women of faith and makes a very challenging comment (vv. 13–14):

> *All these people were still living by faith when they died. They did not receive the things promised; they only saw them and welcomed them from a distance, admitting that they were foreigners and strangers on earth. People who say such things show that they are looking for a country of their own.*

- Living the story
  "*All these people were still living by faith when they died.*"

  People like you and me, unnamed in Hebrews 11, yet known and loved by God and who lived lives loving God and believing in him.

- Listening to the story
  "*They did not receive the things promised; they only saw them and welcomed them from a distance*"

  They listened to the promises of God and believed he would fulfil them even if that meant they were not fulfilled in their lifetime. Amazing!

- Telling the story
  "*admitting that they were foreigners and strangers on earth. People who say such things show that they are looking for a country of their own.*"

  They told the story about their true home with God and living there one day in a new heaven and new earth.

I have seen Hebrews 11:13–14 lived, listened to, and told by someone very close to me. My brother-in-law was a pastor of a large church. In the space of two or three years, he went through suffering that reminded me of the story of Job in the Old Testament. He lost his home, his ministry, his emotional health, his income. Then one day, when he was talking with his family, they noticed his words did not make sense. That was when doctors discovered that he had a brain tumour. It wasn't long before he lost the ability to speak. He died in less than a year. As we prepared for his funeral, his wife told me that, as a couple, they often talked about Hebrews 11:13–14. My brother-in-law, while living, listened to the story of God and he told it through his life. As the cancer grew he gradually lost the ability to speak until he could say just one sentence: "It's all good." Towards the end of his life, when he could not say even that sentence, he could still say it with his eyes and by the peaceful way he endured the cancer. Living the story, listening to the story and telling the story. It is not just something preachers do in the pulpit; it is something we must do in all of life.

That is Hebrews 11. I encourage you to examine other stories in the Bible and in the lives of other people you encounter, and look for this pattern of living, listening and telling being played out. Here are some other examples:

Bible Character/ Event	Living the Story	Listening to the Story	Telling the Story
Moses (Exod 3)	Moses is living as a shepherd in the wilderness.	The Lord appears to Moses in a burning bush and Moses listens to God say that he has heard the cry of his people.	Moses is given a message for the Israelites. He is to tell them the Lord has heard them and will bring them into a new land.
Israel (Exod 6–15)	Israel live preparing to leave their life as slaves and the 10 plagues come upon Egypt (Exod 6–11).	Israel listen to Moses teaching them the Passover meal for the very first time; understanding that God is freeing them (Exod 12).	Israel tell their joyful story of freedom by singing the song of victory after crossing the Red Sea (Exod 15).
Paralyzed Man (Mark 2:1–12)	A paralyzed man is carried by four friends to Jesus (Mark 2:1–4). He is totally dependent on his friends. This is the story he lives.	The man listens as Jesus tell him a new story – his sins are forgiven and he is healed (Mark 2:5–11).	Everyone has a story to tell. They are amazed and praise God (Mark 2:12).

Bible Character/ Event	Living the Story	Listening to the Story	Telling the Story
Mary (Luke 1:26–38; 46–44)	Mary is living the story of a young woman preparing for her marriage to Joseph (Luke 1:26–28).	She listens to the story the angel Gabriel tells. She has found favour with God and she will bear a Son. His kingdom will have no end (Luke 1:30–33).	Mary tells her story in a wonderful song of joy and victory (Luke 1:46–55).
Zacchaeus (Luke 19:1–10)	The story Zacchaeus is living is one which causes hardship for others. He is a chief tax collector and very rich (Luke 19:2–3).	One day Zacchaeus begins to listen to a new story. Jesus tells him to come down from the tree because Jesus wants to stay at his house (Luke 19:5).	Zacchaeus has a new story to tell because of Jesus. He gives to the poor and repays those he has cheated four times what he took (Luke 19:8–10).

Think about your own life. At times you have lived and told stories which are the fruit of you faithfully and obediently listening to the story of God through the Bible. But at other times, the story you live and tell is sinful because you have not listened to the story of Jesus, the great story of love and salvation.

We have looked at examples of people in the Bible living, listening and telling a story through their lives. However, one story in the Bible is my favourite example because of the way it shows us the power of listening to Jesus – how it changes the story we live and the story we tell. This story will be our guide for the rest of our time together in this book.

Living a story, listening to a story, telling a story. Preacher, are you ready?

Questions for Life

Do you really know which story you are listening to? Think about your life, about the story you live and the story you tell. This will reveal which story you are *really* listening to.

2

The Story of Jesus' Life

Luke 24:13–35

¹³ Now that same day two of them were going to a village called Emmaus, about seven miles from Jerusalem. ¹⁴ They were talking with each other about everything that had happened. ¹⁵ As they talked and discussed these things with each other, Jesus himself came up and walked along with them; ¹⁶ but they were kept from recognizing him.

¹⁷ He asked them, "What are you discussing together as you walk along?"

They stood still, their faces downcast. ¹⁸ One of them, named Cleopas, asked him, "Are you the only one visiting Jerusalem who does not know the things that have happened there in these days?"

¹⁹ "What things?" he asked.

"About Jesus of Nazareth," they replied. "He was a prophet, powerful in word and deed before God and all the people. ²⁰ The chief priests and our rulers handed him over to be sentenced to death, and they crucified him; ²¹ but we had hoped that he was the one who was going to redeem Israel. And what is more, it is the third day since all this took place. ²² In addition, some of our women amazed us. They went to the tomb early this morning ²³ but didn't find his body. They came and told us that they had seen a vision of angels, who said he was alive. ²⁴ Then some of our companions went to the tomb and found it just as the women had said, but they did not see Jesus."

²⁵ He said to them, "How foolish you are, and how slow to believe all that the prophets have spoken! ²⁶ Did not the Messiah

have to suffer these things and then enter his glory?" [27] And beginning with Moses and all the Prophets, he explained to them what was said in all the Scriptures concerning himself.

[28] As they approached the village to which they were going, Jesus continued on as if he were going farther. [29] But they urged him strongly, "Stay with us, for it is nearly evening; the day is almost over." So he went in to stay with them.

[30] When he was at the table with them, he took bread, gave thanks, broke it and began to give it to them. [31] Then their eyes were opened and they recognized him, and he disappeared from their sight. [32] They asked each other, "Were not our hearts burning within us while he talked with us on the road and opened the Scriptures to us?"

[33] They got up and returned at once to Jerusalem. There they found the Eleven and those with them, assembled together [34] and saying, "It is true! The Lord has risen and has appeared to Simon." [35] Then the two told what had happened on the way, and how Jesus was recognized by them when he broke the bread.

We have been seeing that people's lives can be described as living a story, listening to a story and telling a story. We have seen that the challenge for preachers is to faithfully tell God's story so that it is the story people live by, listen to and tell. We have seen this pattern present in the lives of the men and women in the Scriptures. Of all the examples of this in the Bible, there is one which is very helpful for us as preachers. It happened on the day Jesus rose from the dead. We know the story simply as the road to Emmaus (Luke 24:13–35). This story is a perfect "preacher's story," because it helps us reflect on the story we are living, listening to and telling. It shows us the importance of first listening carefully to Jesus' story through the Scriptures and how that then changes the story we live and tell.

Living the Story (Luke 24:13–24)

On the first Easter Sunday, two disciples are walking on the road from Jerusalem to a small village named Emmaus. They are sad and shocked because Jesus is gone. They did not expect the things that happened to him. Life is hard. All they had hoped about Jesus seems to be gone. They thought that he would rescue Israel from the Romans and make Israel great as in the days of King David. Now what? They walk and talk (vv. 13–14). They are trying to understand, but are coming up with no answers. Trying to understand what happened to Jesus is too hard.

Then they are joined by a fellow traveller they do not recognize. He asks a question that is so unexpected they stop walking (v. 17). He asks, "What are you discussing together as you walk along?" How could anyone *not* know everything that had happened over the past three days? But this man doesn't seem to know. The two disciples are amazed. And so they begin to tell this mystery traveller all about Jesus of Nazareth (vv. 19–24).

If you carefully read what they say, you will notice they actually tell the gospel, the good news of Jesus Christ. Even though they do not understand it or, at that time, really believe it. They even speak of the resurrection (vv. 22–24). We see two sad and confused disciples who believe and hope in Jesus of Nazareth *but* who think and feel Jesus is no longer with them, even though he is.

This is the story these two disciples were living on that first Easter Sunday.

I wonder whether the story being lived in Luke 24:13–24 is a story you live? Even though you can preach the story of Jesus that his followers told (vv. 19–24), do you sometimes feel as if Jesus is not present in your life? I wonder whether at times you "walk the road" and feel sad and confused like the two disciples in this story. I wonder whether there are times in your life when you do not recognize who is walking with you through life. Sometimes our sadness and pain, the story that we live, makes it hard for us to see and hear Jesus.

Once my wife and I visited a woman of deep and beautiful faith in Christ. As we sat with her she wept and said, "God has forgotten me." The story she was living was one of deep pain. She was tired of the pain, pain that attacked every area of her life. She was suffering physical pain from a disease that very nearly killed her. She was suffering emotional pain from seeing her family suffer. She was suffering from a heart wounded by the sudden death of her husband a few years before. And now she was suffering from the pain of confusion, because she could not hear God. Could not feel God. Could not see God. "God has forgotten me." I think the two disciples on the road to Emmaus felt the same kind of feelings. What do you say to that? How do you *preach* to that? And what if, as a preacher, you find yourself feeling and saying the same thing? "God has forgotten me."

The book of Psalms contains many prayers that reflect this kind of terrible loneliness:

> I say to God my Rock,
>> "Why have you forgotten me?
>> Why must I go about mourning,
>> oppressed by the enemy?" (Ps 42:9)

The story of the road to Emmaus teaches us that there are times when even the people closest to Jesus walk in darkness. Even though the promise is that God will never leave us or forsake us (Heb 13:5), at times we *feel* like he is not there.

This is the kind of life many people are living. They often do so in quiet pain and despair.

I have believed in God ever since I can remember. One Friday night, when I was about ten years old, I was suddenly hit with a terrible thought: "God doesn't exist." I don't know why the thought came into my head, but I was terribly afraid. Suddenly a great darkness fell upon me. Even though it wasn't true, I was faced with the awful thought that God wasn't there. So for two or so days, I prayed and prayed, even though a part of me was saying "You are praying into nothingness. God is not there!" But I kept praying and hoping, hoping and praying. Then, on Sunday afternoon, the darkness lifted and light flooded my life again, as quickly and unexpectedly as the darkness had come upon me. The sense and presence of God returned. I felt such relief and peace.

In your life as a preacher you will go through times of sadness and joy, dark and light, sin and forgiveness, blindness and vision, discouragement and encouragement, doubt and belief, sickness and healing. This will be the story you will live. Your story will be exactly like the experience of the two who walked with Jesus on the road to Emmaus. You will still know the story of Jesus of Nazareth. You will still be living your story trying to follow Jesus. But there will be times when you might not be able to recognize the presence of Jesus as clearly as at other times. And just like the two in Luke 24, you will stand still on the road with your face downcast (v. 17).

Preaching the story of Jesus when you are sad like that is not easy. I was once stopped in my tracks as a preacher. I had been teaching preaching in a Bible college for a few years. A new principal started at the college, and he asked to listen to two of my sermons. Afterwards he told me, "The problem with your sermons is that people leave thinking more about themselves than about Jesus." I was crushed in spirit, not because he was wrong but because I realized he was right. My sermons did not really preach Jesus in a way that taught how Jesus fulfils all of Scripture and fulfils all of life. I was deeply sad and ashamed. But the principal taught me how to listen to the story.

Listening to the Story (Luke 24:25–31)

After the two on the road to Emmaus tell Jesus "his story" (vv. 19–24) in their way, he tells them "his story" (v. 27) in his way. Jesus begins "with Moses and all the Prophets." He explains how he fulfils the promises of God. Jesus himself tells them the story of "Jesus of the whole Bible." He shows them how all the events and stories in the Old Testament are signposts pointing towards him.

Did you notice the question Jesus asks these two disciples? When he first joins them as they walk, he asks, "What are you discussing together as you walk along?" As we have seen, that is a surprising question for them, but it is a warm question. A friendly question. But now Jesus asks another question, and it is a tough one: "How foolish you are, and how slow to believe all that the prophets have spoken! Did not the Messiah have to suffer these things and then enter his glory?" (vv. 25–26). In other words, he tells them they have not been listening to the story carefully, just as the principal of the Bible college pointed out to me that I had not been listening to the story of Jesus carefully. Remember, if we do not listen to the story carefully, we will not live the story faithfully or tell the story properly. This is why preachers must learn to listen.

The part of the story of Jesus that the two disciples needed to listen to most was that the Messiah had to suffer. In the Gospels, whenever Jesus spoke about his suffering, death and resurrection, no one understood what he meant (e.g. Mark 8:31–33). They believed God would send them a deliverer (the Messiah), but they thought he would be a king like King David of the Old Testament. They thought the Messiah would again make them a great nation with a mighty army. But Jesus was never going to be that kind of king. Jesus' kingdom was much more powerful than any kingdom Israel or any other nation on earth had known or will ever know. Jesus' kingdom is one of justice, mercy and love, but it is not of this world. The kingdom of God does things differently from any other kingdom. In the kingdom of God, the King dies to conquer evil and sin. Imagine Moses going to the Israelites when they were slaves in Egypt and saying, "I am from God. I am here to lead you out of slavery. I will rescue you. And the way I will do that is to hand myself over to Pharaoh and the Egyptians, and they will kill me. That is how I will free you." Such a plan just would not make sense. Yet Jesus, the Son of God, dying and rising again, was God's plan to save the world and to free us from the slavery of sin.

"How foolish you are, and how slow to believe all that the prophets have spoken! Did not the Messiah have to suffer these things and then enter his glory?" It's easy for us to understand Jesus had to suffer and die for our sin, because we can read the Scriptures and see the witness of God's people to God's plan. But maybe today, as preachers, we too are still "foolish" and "slow to believe." Maybe, like the two disciples in Luke 24, we struggle with how suffering has a place in the life of faith as believers in Christ. Maybe this is why we are sometimes deaf to the story of Jesus and fail to listen to his story.

As a pastor in what is known as the Western world, I regularly see Christians suffering awful problems. They struggle with burdens such as terrible sickness or broken relationships with those they love. However in the West, unlike other parts of the world, we do not experience physical violence for our faith in Christ. As a pastor, one of the things that surprises me is that, although Christians know that one day everyone will die, some live as if death will never happen to them or their family. I am surprised that when death does come, it can greatly damage their faith. They seem shocked. They stop listening to the story of Jesus.

The story of Jesus is about suffering and glory. Many disciples of Jesus today are standing still on the "road to Emmaus" with their faces downcast. They cannot make sense of the pain and hurt they are feeling, and they cannot sense Jesus in their life. This is one reason why you as a preacher must listen to the story carefully and deeply, so you can tell the story to people – so that they can live the story and start walking again in the presence of Jesus. As preachers, we must learn to listen to the story of Jesus "beginning with Moses and all the Prophets." It is your job as a preacher to listen to the story of Jesus through the Scriptures. When you listen, you are equipped to tell it, and so help people change the story they are living and telling.

Once my wife and I were in a foreign city for the first time. One night, as we walked through the city, we came across a beautiful cathedral. We wanted to go inside, so we walked all around the cathedral looking for a way in. We tried every door we came to, but they were all locked. As we tried each door, we could hear from within the most beautiful music and singing. In fact, we thought that the music was a recording, because it seemed too perfect to be live. We came to the last door we could try. We discovered it too was locked, but there was a keyhole in the door. I bent down and looked inside. I could see the inside of the cathedral lit up with wonderful yellow light and on the far side a choir singing. Through the keyhole I could see *some* of the inside of the cathedral but not all of it. I could see *some* of the choir but not everyone.

As we sat outside the door, I heard another sound, the sound of the city's peak hour traffic with car horns and engines. People were either driving home after working all day or driving into the city for the night. I realized that these people could not hear what I could hear and had not seen what I had seen. The sound of the cars was the sound of people hurrying and people under pressure. I was struck by the contrast of the sounds from the cathedral and the sounds from the city. One sound was the sound of worship of God, and the other sound was the sound of the burden of life.

As preachers it is our job to listen to the "sounds from the cathedral" and make this message known to those who are listening to the "sounds of life." As preachers, we have looked through the keyhole and seen a little bit of the kingdom of God. As preachers, we sit at the door of God's temple and listen to the sounds from within. As preachers, we tell others what we have seen and heard through listening to the story of Jesus. If we listen well, we will have wonderful stories to tell others.

The two disciples on the road to Emmaus walk with Jesus. He begins his journey with them by asking what they are talking about as they walk along. He gives them something new to talk about: an amazing Bible study showing them how the Messiah is present in all the stories from the beginning of the Bible. They listen and their hearts change. We could say that Jesus showed them how to look through the keyhole and how to listen to the music and singing from within the great story of the Bible.

Then the two disciples arrive at the village, and it is nearly evening. Their travelling companion looks as if he is going to keep on walking, but they want to hear more. They want to keep listening to him, so they urge him to stay. He accepts their invitation and joins them at the table and breaks bread. It is in this moment they recognize him and he then disappears from their sight (vv. 30–31).

They are not the same people who began their journey a few hours before. The story they have been living is now different because of the story they have been listening to. "They asked each other, 'Were not our hearts burning within us while he talked with us on the road and opened the Scriptures to us?'" (v. 32). I love that. Hearts that were frightened are now hearts on fire, and heavy spirits are now hallelujah spirits.

I find what these two disciples do next exciting. They walk the seven miles back to Jerusalem at night. They cannot wait until morning. Why? Because now they have a story to tell! Now they have a new story to live – all because of the story they have just listened to. Everything is different now. So they return to Jerusalem at a dangerous time of the day (night) and at a dangerous time to be a disciple of Jesus (days after Jesus has been crucified). Let's now consider the story they tell.

Telling the Story (Luke 24:32–35)

Our two friends arrive back in Jerusalem and they find the eleven disciples and the others who are with them. When they join the others, they discover something wonderful. Luke describes what happens when the two disciples arrive where the Eleven are (vv. 33–35):

> They got up and returned at once to Jerusalem. There they found the Eleven and those with them, assembled together and saying, "It is true! The Lord has risen and has appeared to Simon." Then the two told what had happened on the way, and how Jesus was recognized by them when he broke the bread.

When the two arrive, those in Jerusalem are already telling the story about Jesus' resurrection to each other. "It is true! The Lord has risen and has appeared to Simon" (Luke 24:34).

The two from the road to Emmaus arrive back to Jerusalem and discover the others have also been listening to the new amazing story of the resurrection of Jesus. The others have already begun telling a new story. The two from the road to Emmaus join in and "then the two told what had happened on the way, and how Jesus was recognized by them when he broke the bread" (Luke 24:35). The resurrected presence of Jesus has changed the story the disciples and believers were telling.

Earlier I mentioned that I pastored a church for a number of years. Once I was away from the church for three months. I was excited about returning to the church and telling my brothers and sisters in Christ all that had happened in my life while I was away. I was looking forward to "telling the story." When I returned and met with the leaders of the church, it was just like the ending of Luke 24:13–35. Not only did I have a fresh and deeper story to tell about

Jesus, so did they. They talked about God's presence in prayer meetings and worship services. They talked about a new focus on evangelism and working in the neighbourhood. They talked about preaching the gospel and treating each other with more grace. They talked about wanting to be more mature in living out the good news of Jesus Christ and doing things in a new way. They talked about "thorns in the flesh," but also about discovering that God's "grace is sufficient." It was wonderful. They were telling me how they had met with the resurrected Christ. When they finished, I told them how Christ had met with me over the past three months. I talked about the things I had learnt as I had listened to the story of Jesus over the time I had been away. We told our stories with Jesus at the centre of it all.

As a preacher, the way you tell the story is the fruit of how you listen to Jesus and the message of the Scriptures. As you begin to understand how Jesus fulfils all of Scripture, your heart will burn within you. When you see how the Old Testament promises so much and then how Jesus is the fulfilment of those promises, the Bible begins to make more sense. We begin to see and understand how the Scriptures are telling the great single story of God rescuing people through Jesus Christ. Life begins to make more sense. Your ministry and service begin to make more sense. The story you tell begins to make more sense. Jesus is at the centre of our life, ministry and message. You will find you have more courage in telling the story. You will be more prepared to go to places you were afraid of in the past. You will be prepared to speak to people you were afraid of in the past.

Let me tell you about Sadie. Sadie is a young woman who loves Jesus. But Sadie does not love standing before groups of people and speaking. She would rather do anything other than that. One day Sadie felt called by God to go on a short mission trip to South Asia. Over the months before her trip, she listened to the story of Jesus in new ways. She heard someone tell the message this way: "Don't miss out on the 'you' God is dreaming of." That saying got into her soul. She began to explore the vision of God for her life. So even though she never liked standing before groups of people and talking, she began to do so more and more. Before she left on the trip, she would speak to the church during our worship services. She would bear witness to the new work Jesus was doing in her life. She began to talk about her planned trip to the people she worked with each day. As a result of listening to Jesus' story, when she went to South Asia, she told her story before a group of preachers. I was there and heard it myself. It was incredible! A few months after she returned home, she had to speak at a very large wedding. She spoke about

Jesus. She honoured God before hundreds of people. I believe that God is gently creating a preacher in this young disciple of his. Why do I believe this? Because she listened to the story and has been empowered to tell the story. Listening to Jesus' story is now changing how she wants to live the story and tell the story. She has shown bravery by going to another country and culture and doing something that scares her. But God is with her and is using her to tell his story.

I want you to imagine that, as a preacher, you walk up and down the road to Emmaus. I want you to imagine that your work on that road is to tell the story to the sad and confused disciples you encounter there, to the people who believe in Jesus but are unable to sense his presence with them. Your role as a preacher is to follow Jesus' example and walk with those people and open the Scriptures up to them so that they can see Christ. Your role as a preacher is to tell them the story of Jesus from the Scriptures, so that their hearts will burn within them.

One day I decided that I needed to renew my promise to the church that I pastored. I decided that I could not do it in any other way than to use the road to Emmaus as my guide. So I stood before the people and told them that I was going to tell them the story. This is what I said:

> I will wait on the road to Emmaus and help you understand and experience the story. I will work hard to help you walk that road as you do so with Christ, trying to make sense of it all again, trying to apply the story to whatever you encounter on that road. Whenever. However. I offer myself to you to help you experience the presence of the resurrected Christ, through the breaking of bread and through the opening of the Scriptures. I offer myself to you to work hard in constantly bringing you this story, so that your heart will burn with the revelation of what God has done in Christ and what this resurrection news means today. . . . I will wait on the road to Emmaus and there will study the Scriptures and teach you, so that you will increasingly recognize your loving resurrected companion on the road – no matter how bright the day or dark the night.

After I said that, we sang a final song, and the worship service finished. As I walked from the front of the church where I had been speaking, a woman got out of her seat and stood in my way. She is not the kind of person to say a lot about her faith and neither is she the kind of person to show much emotion.

But on this day, as she blocked my path, she said with deep meaning, "Thank you." Then she hugged me. I had told the story, and she had heard it. Her heart changed in Christ.

Questions for Life

Think about the story you are living in Christ. What would Jesus say to you if it had been you on the road to Emmaus?

Think about the story you are listening to in Christ. What would Jesus most need to say to you about himself from the Scriptures if you had been on the road to Emmaus?

Think about the story you are telling in Christ. What would you most need to say after listening to Jesus on the road to Emmaus?

3

Listening to the Story:
On the Road to Emmaus
Part 1 – *Lectio Divina*

We have seen that we are all living, listening and telling a story throughout our lives. We have seen how the story of the road to Emmaus is helpful in guiding preachers in their ministry of opening the Scriptures for others. We have also seen that listening to the story of Jesus can lead people to change the story they live and tell. But how can we really live as if we are on the road to Emmaus 2000 years after it happened? How can we place ourselves on that road listening to Jesus opening the Scriptures to us? How can we really listen to the Spirit, so we can preach (tell) the story in such a way that people's hearts burn within them?

We can pray Scripture in two ways that help us listen to the story of God. Both ways of praying have been used by Christians around the world for hundreds of years. Both help place us in the Bible text in such a way that we find ourselves eyewitnesses to the story of God. Both ways enable us to pray the text in such a way that we clothe ourselves with the message of Scripture. The ways of praying are called *lectio divina* and Ignatian Gospel Contemplation. You need to remember one important thing: pray, using either of these methods, *before* you do any other kind of preparation or study for your sermon. Pray the text, *then* study the text. This will ensure you listen to the story before telling it.

Let's begin with *lectio divina*.

Lectio divina is a Latin term that simply means "divine reading." *Lectio divina* has been used by Christians for over 1500 years. This way of reading and praying the Bible has helped people who struggle with being distracted when they pray. It has also been useful when people do not have their own copies of the Bible. In this practice, one person reads Scripture aloud, and others hear the Word of God and then pray the Bible passage. *Lectio divina* is a wonderful way to listen to the story of God. It is easy to learn and a powerful habit to include in your sermon preparation.

Lectio divina has four parts:

1. *Lectio* (reading)
   Read the Bible passage aloud, listening for one word, phrase or sentence that catches your attention.

2. *Meditatio* (meditation)
   Think about that one word, phrase or sentence.

3. *Oratio* (response)
   Pray about what you have thought about.

4. *Contemplatio* (contemplation)
   Be quiet and still with God.

The prayer looks easy. Just go through the steps in order: 1-2-3-4. But the Spirit can also mix things up. So as you read aloud (*lectio*), an important thought might come into your mind (*mediatio*). Or as you meditate, you might suddenly want to pray (*oratio*) a prayer of worship.

Lectio divina is like cooking a meal with four ingredients. You place all of them into the pot, and they begin to work together to create a beautiful meal. Or think of the prayer as a dance with four different movements or steps. At the beginning, when you are learning the dance, you take each step carefully, but once you are used to all the steps, they become one smooth dance. Or think of a rainbow. You can see the different colours, but you are also amazed at the whole sight. Or imagine picking up a piece of delicious fruit and taking a bite (*lectio*). Then you chew on it and enjoy the beautiful flavour (*meditatio*). You swallow the piece of fruit and comment about how tasty it was (*oratio*). Finally, your body is satisfied by being fed such healthy food (*contemplatio*).

Lectio divina can also be likened to farming. Think of a crop that is harvested. The crop did not just appear. Before it was ready to harvest, it required seed, soil, sun and rain. Each is important, but only together do they bring forth the harvest. In fact, Jesus uses the example of farming in one of the parables about the kingdom of God (Mark 4:26–29):

> He also said, "This is what the kingdom of God is like. A man scatters seed on the ground. Night and day, whether he sleeps or gets up, the seed sprouts and grows, though he does not know how. All by itself the soil produces grain – first the stalk, then the head, then the full kernel in the head. As soon as the grain is ripe, he puts the sickle to it, because the harvest has come."

Did you notice that in this parable, Jesus said: "*All by itself* the soil produces . . ." As you pray a passage from the Bible using *lectio divina*, you will find that the spiritual harvest will take place "all by itself." When you begin your prayer using *lectio divina*, God is waiting for you and the Spirit is at work. God's action in the time of prayer, not your action, is the main thing. So just as "all by itself the soil produces," so it is with this prayer. When I studied at Bible college I loved what one of my teachers used to say about this way of praying: "Don't make it happen; see what happens."

Let's begin then. Remember, this way of praying is the first part of your sermon preparation. This is how we begin to listen to the story.

Choose the Bible Passage You Want to Preach From

When you pray using *lectio divina*, you can choose any type of passage from the Bible, although it is best not to use *lectio divina* to pray through a story in the Bible (e.g. one of the events in the life of Jesus). Ignatian Gospel Contemplation is better suited to those texts. We will look at that kind of prayer in the next chapter.

Prepare for *lectio divina* by quietly asking the Holy Spirit to help you as you pray.

Lectio: Read Aloud

Once you have chosen the passage from the Bible that you want to preach from, begin reading it aloud and slowly. As you read aloud, listen for one word, phrase or sentence that catches your attention. You might hear this word, phrase or sentence the first time you read the passage or not until the third time you read it. Reading the passage repeatedly is important. Read until you hear *the* word that God wants you to hear during this time of prayer.

When you use *lectio divina* you are meeting with a Person, not simply reading and listening to words. Jesus is present, helping you hear what he wants you to say through Scripture. Take Psalm 23 as an example. If you were reading this passage, you might find "shepherd" (v. 1) is the word for you. Or maybe the words "he makes me lie down" (v. 2) suddenly take on special meaning as you read. Or the Spirit wants you to hear the words "even though I walk through the darkest valley" (v. 4). The important thing is to listen and be aware as you read aloud to yourself. God knows what you need to hear when you pray. Be still and quiet in spirit as you slowly and carefully read the words of Scripture. The word or words for you will become very obvious. Do not be anxious about whether you will hear them. You will. Expect to hear God speak.

I used to be a police chaplain. A police chaplain helps the police and their families in much the same way a pastor cares for his or her congregation. I would offer counselling, provide training to help police cope with their work, and conduct weddings and funerals. I would also regularly go out with the police on night patrol. One night I went out with a police sergeant and a few police officers. They had to go into a home and take the children away because of a family problem. When the people realized that the children were being taken to another family member, things became very difficult. People began shouting and the situation became very emotional and loud.

While this was happening I noticed the sergeant turn to one side and answer his radio. I was amazed. I could not believe that, with all the noise, he had been able to hear his call sign and answer his radio. His radio was not even turned up very loud. Later I asked him how he had heard his radio in all the confusion. He said, "Have you ever been in a crowded room and heard one of your children call your name? You hear their voice and your name. Hearing my call sign over the radio is no different. I'm listening for it."

When you are reading aloud, you are listening for the voice of God. Amid the noise outside your window or thoughts that do not relate to what you are reading, you are listening for the voice of God speaking to you just one word from the passage you are reading or just a few words of a sentence. That is all. When you hear that word or words, it will feel as if you are hearing your name. Within you, you will sense a response just as if your very name had been called. You will find you have become more alert and even more interested. Trust in God that he will speak.

Meditatio: Think Deeply

Once you have heard the one word or a few words from the passage you are reading aloud, you begin the next part of the prayer, *meditatio*. *Meditatio* is the time when you begin to think about what you have heard. Let's keep using Psalm 23 as an example. Let's say that on the second reading of Psalm 23, when you read "Even though I walk through the darkest valley, I will fear no evil, for you are with me; your rod and your staff, they comfort me" (v. 4), the word "comfort" really took hold of you.

Now you begin to meditate on this word and think about why, of all the words you have just heard from Psalm 23, this one word is special today. Ask yourself questions about the word "comfort." What is happening in my life that the word "comfort" is the word God wants me to hear? What is happening in the life of my church that this word is important? When I read all of Psalm 23, what place does comfort play in the whole psalm? In the verse where comfort appears, there is also the mention of a dark valley and evil. Is this why God is speaking to me about comfort? Verse 4 says that in the darkest valley "I will fear no evil" because God promises to comfort me. Have I experienced a lack of fear because of the presence of God's comfort? When I think of the word "comfort," where else in Scripture does my mind go to? How do I comfort others? Do I know anyone who really needs comfort right now? In what ways did Jesus comfort people? How does the word "comfort" make me feel? Do I feel the presence of comfort from God or the absence of it? These are some of the many questions you can ask. Your own questions will come to mind; you will not need to look for them. The Spirit is with you and will guide you during this time.

Imagine that the word "comfort" (or whatever word or phrase from the reading caught your attention) is like a good friend who has come to visit you in your home. You answer the door and invite your friend in, and you sit together and talk. You open your home to your friend, and your life is better for having this time with your friend. For some of the time you will speak, some of the time you will listen, and some of the time you will simply sit in silence. Through your time together you get to know each other better. So it is when you sit with your word (in this case "comfort") during *meditatio*.

During this part of *lectio divina*, writing down what you are thinking can be helpful. Sometimes something special will come to your mind, but with all the other thoughts in your head, you can easily forget it. So writing down your questions, answers and thoughts can help you to remember what God was saying to you and bring that message to your mind later on. Remember, too, that you are praying in this way to prepare to preach, so some of your thoughts and questions will become part of your sermon later on. You will find writing down what is happening as you do *lectio divina* will help your sermon writing after you have prayed.

Oratio: Pray Honestly

After having thought and wrestled with the word God has spoken to you, you now respond. Through *lectio* and *meditatio*, God has spoken, and now you answer him. You will discover that what you want to say to God will feel quite natural. The kind of prayer, your response to God's word to you, will have formed during *meditatio*. The kind of response could be anything. For example, you might be filled with a sense of thankfulness about what God has said and what he has done in your life. Or you might find yourself offering a prayer asking God to meet a need in your life or in the life of someone you know (a prayer of intercession). Meditating on the passage may have helped you see a need much more clearly, and so you now pray about that. Or you may be filled with a sense of worship, and this is your response. You praise God and worship him in prayer. Sometimes the way God speaks through *lectio* and *meditatio* leads you to pray a prayer of confession to him. His word could have exposed an area in your life that needs to change. Your prayer could be one of confessing, surrendering, and seeking his forgiveness. The prayer you pray could be a mixture of all these kinds of prayers. The possibilities for our response are endless.

If we stay with the word "comfort" (Ps 23:4) as an example, you may find that, through thinking about that word and asking questions about it, your prayer is:

> Lord God. You are the shepherd who leads me and is with me. I see now that I have been in dark valleys, and I have been afraid for a long time. I now see that you protect me and comfort me. I have been in darkness and fear for so long that I realize I have been blind and deaf to your presence. Today, reading and hearing about your comfort has soothed my soul and given me hope again. Thank you!

Or the response (*oratio*) might be: "Lord, help me to be more aware of your comfort than of the dark valley and my fear."

I have discovered something special about *oratio* when I use *lectio divina* as part of my sermon preparation. When we write a sermon, we always build the sermon around one short statement that summarizes the Bible passage and applies it to the listeners. For centuries preachers have been encouraged to work hard in creating this part of the sermon. This statement has been described in many different ways: "the big idea," "the sermon in a sentence," or "the sermon proposition." By beginning with such a statement, the sermon has unity of thought and good direction. I have discovered the response prayed during *oratio* is often the key thought that will be at the centre of the sermon.

Taking the second prayer above as an example, my summary statement for my sermon could be:

> The Shepherd's comfort empowers us in times of darkness and fear.

Sometimes I write the prayer at the top of the page as a reminder as I prepare the rest of the sermon. The prayer flows through all that I study, write and preach concerning that particular Bible passage. This is some of the power of *oratio*.

By now, you have completed a lot of work. What is next? In a word, rest.

Contemplatio: Rest Quietly

The final part of *lectio divina*, called *contemplatio*, is resting in the presence of God. I love this definition of contemplation: I gaze at Jesus, and he gazes at me. Have you ever sat quietly with a good friend? Have you ever been with someone and spoken no words, but you are content in each other's company? This is what *contemplatio* is like as you finish your time of prayer with Jesus. However, *contemplatio* can be the most difficult part of *lectio divina*. People have difficulty simply resting in God's presence, because they feel like they are doing nothing. They struggle because they think they ought to be either saying something or doing something. They struggle because they feel lazy and think they should be busy. They fail to understand that they *are* doing something: they are being with their Lord and Saviour.

In John 15, Jesus spoke about the vine and branches. In verse 5 he says, "I am the vine; you are the branches. If you remain in me and I in you, you will bear much fruit; apart from me you can do nothing." This picture of a vine and branches is a wonderful way to think of *contemplatio*. We abide in Christ and he in us. We sit with Jesus and rest in him. Elsewhere in the Gospel of John, Jesus said "Anyone who loves me will obey my teaching. My Father will love them, and we will come to them and make our home with them" (John 14:23). I love that image of God making his home with us. Again this is a helpful way to think of what happens at this point of *lectio divina*. We are the branches in the vine, gaining life from the source of all life, Jesus Christ, who has just spoken with us. We are the dwelling place of God as we love him and obey his teaching.

We have heard the Spirit speak (*lectio*), we have meditated on the Word of God (*meditatio*), and we have responded with a prayer that has emerged from this time (*oratio*). *Contemplatio* is enjoying the presence of God.

We have listened to the story. When you pray a passage from the Bible using *lectio divina* it is like that moment on the road to Emmaus when the two disciples listened to Jesus talking about how he fulfils Scripture. We listen to his story.

Questions for Life

Choose a Bible passage and pray using *lectio divina*. What did you find easy about listening to the story? What did you find difficult about listening to the story?

4

Listening to the Story: On the Road to Emmaus
Part 2 – Ignatian Gospel Contemplation

If you were given the opportunity to be personally present at any one of the events in Jesus' life, which one would you choose? Would you love to be at Cana and see the surprise on the face of the wine steward and bridegroom when told that the best wine they had ever tasted was ordinary water a few moments before (John 2:1–11)? Or would you choose to be in the crowd of over 5,000 people being fed with a few loaves and fish, and still having plenty left over (Matt 14:13–21)? Maybe you would want to be there that first Christmas night (Luke 2:1–20). Or when Jesus changed Zacchaeus' life (Luke 19:1–10). Or when Jesus told the story about the Good Samaritan to the expert in the law (Luke 10:25–37). Or when he was arrested in the garden of Gethsemane and his power knocked the mob to the ground (John 18:1–14). Could you bear to see him on the cross (Mark 15:21–41)? Would you dare approach his tomb and talk with the angels there and join the weeping Mary as she looked for her Lord (John 20:1–18)? At which event in the life of Jesus would you choose to be present?

Remember, we have been considering how our lives can unfold. How we live a story, listen to a story and tell a story. Imagine the impact of experiencing an event from the life of Jesus (listening to a story). What a difference that could make to the story we live and the story we tell.

In the previous chapter, we learnt one way of listening to the story: *lectio divina. Lectio divina* can be used to pray all the different kinds of passages in the Bible. But for the stories in the Bible (especially stories about Jesus) there is another way of praying: Ignatian Gospel Contemplation. This second way of praying can powerfully place you in the story of Jesus as if you were really there. However, just as when using *lectio divina*, it is important to pray the Scripture *before* you do any other kind of preparation or study for your sermon. Pray the text, *then* study the text. This will ensure you listen to the story before telling it.

When praying the Scriptures using Ignatian Gospel Contemplation there are a few simple steps to guide you:

1. A prayer to start

2. A story to read

3. A place to imagine

4. A grace to desire

5. An event to experience

6. A conversation to have

1. A Prayer to Start (Preparatory Prayer)[1]

Before you even begin to read the Bible passage, the first part of Ignatian Gospel Contemplation is to pray in a very specific way. We can sum it up by quoting Psalm 46:10: "Be still and know that I am God." Quieten your heart and mind and be aware of what is about to take place and why. You are going to prayerfully enter into the story of Jesus so that you may better tell his story through your preaching. "Be still and know that I am God." Be still and be aware of God's love towards you and to all who will hear the message you will preach. Know that he is God; the God of love, grace and truth. Consider how the Bible speaks of the extravagant generosity of God and his abundant kindness. He lavishes his love upon us that we should be called children of God (1 John 3:1). He is the God who has given grace upon grace, and grace in place of grace already given (John 1:16). He is the God who sets us free by his truth (John 8:32). Still yourself in the presence of the God of love, grace and truth. Be still.

---

1. You will notice that each of the headings in this next section has another heading in brackets. For example, A Prayer to Start (Preparatory Prayer). The headings in brackets are the formal headings usually given to each part of the prayer. I include them just in case you read about this kind of prayer in other books and come across such headings.

2.   A Story to Read (1st Prelude – Subject Matter)

The next step is an obvious one. Read the particular gospel story that you are going to preach from. What might not be obvious, though, is *how* you read it. Read it more than once. Often the stories about Jesus are very familiar to us. We have read them a lot and have heard them preached a lot. So, because they are familiar, it is easy for us to become deaf and blind to them. Read and reread the gospel passage until it is fresh in your heart and mind. If the story you are reading appears in more than one of the Gospels, read the other accounts too. Read it as many times as you need to.

Another important way to read the story is to read it aloud. When you read aloud you will say and hear every word the Bible uses to describe the story. When we read silently it is possible to rush over some of the details. When we read aloud it is easier to concentrate on them. Let me give you an example.

Do you recall the passage in Mark 8 where Jesus asks his disciples "Who do people say I am?" (v. 27). The disciples give various answers, and then Jesus asks them, "But what about you? Who do you say I am?" (v. 29). Peter says "You are the Messiah." Then Jesus begins to talk about his suffering, death and resurrection. We read that then "Peter took him aside and began to rebuke him" (v. 32). Let me ask you a question. Without opening your Bible to check, what happened next?

I have asked this very question to a number of different groups and the answer is always the same: "Jesus rebukes Peter and says 'Get behind me Satan.'" Is that your answer too? It is definitely how I would have answered that question – until I read the story aloud and slowly.

One day when preparing a sermon and using Ignatian Gospel Contemplation to pray about this passage, I read Mark 8:27–33 aloud. For the first time ever I noticed that *before* Jesus rebuked Peter, something else happened that is very important. Something that I had never noticed when I read the passage silently many times before.

After Peter rebukes Jesus and *before* Jesus rebukes Peter, we read in verse 33, "But when Jesus turned and looked at his disciples . . ." It is only after doing that that Jesus rebukes Peter. Mark does not explain what Jesus saw or thought when he turned and looked at the disciples. But something clearly happened in that moment. Jesus had been taken aside from the group by Peter and now he looks back at them before replying to Peter. So Jesus' rebuke was not just a response to Peter, it was a response to what he saw on the disciples' faces. He had their well-being in mind too. I wonder what else we miss when we read Scripture quickly and silently in our minds.

Read the story several times and read it aloud.

3. A Place to Imagine (2nd Prelude – Composition of Place)

By now you have read (and heard) the story a number of times. You are ready for the next part of the preparation. Before you really plunge into the prayer, picture the scene in your mind. For instance, let's say you are preaching on the feeding of the 5,000 in Matthew 14:13–21. We read in verse 13 that Jesus "withdrew by boat privately to a solitary place." After the crowds came to him, he told them to sit down on the grass (v 19). Picture in your mind what the "solitary place" is like. Is it near the water? Is it windswept? Is it a lonely grassy hill? Is it a grassy flat area? Are there many trees? The gospel account does not give us a lot of detail about exactly what the place looked like, so we have to imagine what it may have looked like. Don't worry about getting it wrong . . . because you can't. You are imagining a country scene where Jesus performed a miracle. Whether you think that it took place on the side of a grassy hill or on a flat grassy area does not affect what happens in the story. Do not worry if you think you do not have a very good imagination. You do. Truly. If I asked you to tell me about your home I am sure you could describe it to me very well. You need imagination to do that. If I asked you to think of your favourite meal and tell me about it, again I am sure you could. Do not worry about the imagination you think you don't have; enjoy the one you *do* have. Once you have a picture in mind, you are nearly ready to begin the main time of prayer. However, there is one more thing to ask of God first.

4. A Grace to Desire (3rd Prelude – Asking for Desired Grace)

By now you have stilled yourself in the presence of God who loves you deeply. Then you have read and reread the passage from Scripture that you will be preaching from. And, because you have read the story aloud, you have heard the Word of God. You are refreshed and reminded of all the details of the story. Next, you have imagined what the place where this happened looked like. Now you are going to ask God for something special – grace.

In making this request, you are asking for a deep and personal knowledge of Jesus your Lord. You are asking to know him in a greater and deeper way through this experience of prayer. One way of describing this prayer is "asking for desired grace." You are asking God to give you a specific experience of his grace during this particular time of prayer. The grace you are asking for will be different from one person to another. The content of your prayer will be shaped by all that has happened up until this point in your prayer time. From the very first part when you were quiet before God, and then during your reading of the Scripture and imagining the place where the event took place, a desire will have been growing in your heart. You can trust that the Holy Spirit is forming that desire. Whatever need you feel or whatever request is coming into your mind, trust the Holy Spirit's guidance in it all. The Holy Spirit knows what you need and what is needed for the sermon you are preparing.

Just one word of direction about this. The grace that you desire needs to be in keeping with the spirit of the story. So, for example, if the Scripture you are praying is centred on the crucifixion, you would not be praying "Lord, give me a sense of joy as I pray." Your prayer would be more along the lines of "Lord, give me a new awareness of my sin and your great forgiveness." Likewise, if you were praying the Scriptures about the resurrection of Jesus, you would be asking for the grace of joy at Jesus' victory rather than being sorrowful about evil in the world. This prayer of "asking for desired grace" is a humble prayer. We ask for desired grace knowing that God will answer in his way.

5. An Event to Experience (Gospel Contemplation)

Let's remind ourselves of our prayer journey so far.

1. *A prayer to start* – you have stilled yourself in the presence of the God of Love

2. *A story to read* – you have read and reread the gospel story aloud

3. *A place to imagine* – you have imagined what the place looks like where the event in Jesus' life happened

4. *A grace to desire* – you have asked God for desired grace in keeping with the spirit of the story.

Now comes the really fun part. By now you will know the particular Bible story well. You have already imagined the scene of the story. You know where it happened (e.g. on the Sea of Galilee or in the High Priest's courtyard as Peter warms himself by the fire). You know who were there (e.g. the crowds or maybe people like Mary and Martha whose names we know). You know what was said (e.g. someone was asking Jesus a question or the Pharisees were accusing Jesus). You know what happened (e.g. Jesus going missing in Jerusalem when he was twelve years old or Jesus healing someone). You know when it happened (e.g. morning or evening). Of course not all the stories in the Gospels will give all the kinds of details mentioned above, but they will give you enough.

What you do now is play the gospel story in your imagination, as if you were watching it in a movie. Or the way you do when you read a book and picture the people and events in the story. Follow the order of events and dialogue as it appears in Scripture. However, now you enter the story. You imagine that you were actually there when the story happened. You could imagine you are one of the crowd. Or one of the disciples. Or you could be someone standing off to one side and just watching and listening to everything that happens. Now you prayerfully imagine the event in Jesus' life *as if you were really there.* Use your five physical senses to help you experience the story in your imagination. To help you do this, you can ask yourself the following questions:[2]

What do I see?

Look at the people and what they are doing. What does the demon-possessed man in look like when he is so tormented he can break chains (Mark 5:1–20)? And what does he look like when he is clothed and in his right mind after the power of Jesus has delivered him? What does the woman who had been bleeding for twelve years look like when Jesus asks who had touched him and she comes forward trembling with fear (Mark 5:33–34)? What does Jesus look like when he is on the Mount of Transfiguration (Mark 9:2–10)? How is the crowd acting as Zacchaeus tries to see over and through them to catch a glimpse of Jesus (Luke 19:1–10)? What does Judas' face look like when he takes the bread and Satan enters into him (John 13:26–27)? What does the mob look like as they come to arrest Jesus (John 18:1–13)? What do the angels look like at the empty tomb (John 20:11–13)?

---

2. I have used examples from a wide range of stories from the life of Jesus to illustrate the different ways you can use your physical senses to help your imagination. When you are praying as part of your sermon preparation, you will be focused on just one story.

What do I hear?

Listen to Jesus and others as they speak in the story. Listen to what they are saying. Listen to the other sounds in the story. Maybe you can hear the sounds of the marketplace, for example. Or if you are praying the story of Jesus cleansing the temple (John 2:13–22) imagine all the sounds you would hear. What do the angels sound like on that first Christmas night as they celebrate the birth of the King (Luke 2:13–14)? Can you hear the crowds crying out "Hosanna in the highest! Blessed is he who comes in the name of the Lord!" as Jesus rides into Jerusalem (Matt 21:9–10)? What do the two thieves crucified on either side of Jesus sound like as one taunts him and the other defends him (Luke 23:39–43)?

What do I touch?

Some stories have Jesus touching the eyes of a blind man. We read about the woman who wept at the feet of Jesus and dried them with her hair (Luke 7:36–50). What about Thomas being invited by the resurrected Jesus to touch the wounds on his side and hands (John 20:24–29)? Different stories give the opportunity to feel a touch or to touch someone or something. For example, maybe you are one of the disciples dragging in a huge, miraculous catch of fish (John 21:6). Do you feel the net as you grip and strain to pull it on board? Do you feel the fish as they jump around in the boat? Do you feel the water sloshing over the side of the boat as it nearly sinks because there are so many fish? Are you praying the story in John 13 when Jesus washes his disciples' feet? What does his touch feel like as he cleans the dirt and grime off your feet?

What do I taste?

One Sabbath Jesus and his disciples were walking through grain fields when the disciples began eating the heads of grain (Matt 12:1–8). Join them and taste the grain (while listening to Jesus' reply to the Pharisees' angry complaint about it). What does that wine taste like at Cana (John 2:1–11)? Did you taste some of the loaves and fish at the feeding of the 5,000 (Luke 9:10–17)? Or the bread and wine at the Last Supper (Matt 26:17–30)? What about the fish on hot coals and the bread that Jesus prepares on the shores of the Sea of Galilee (John 21:1–14)?

What do I smell?

When Jesus was born the wise men from the East brought gifts. Can you smell the frankincense and myrrh (Matt 2:11)? We read about Mary anointing Jesus at Bethany and the fragrance of the perfume filling the house (John 12:1–8). What is that like? Martha works in the kitchen preparing food for everyone while Mary sits at the feet of Jesus (Luke 10:38–42). Does the smells of the food waft into the room where Jesus is talking and Mary is listening? Luke 24 begins with the women going to the tomb with spices they had prepared for Jesus' body. What is the aroma of those spices like as it drifts through the garden very early on that first Easter morning?

Using your five physical senses helps you imagine the scene as you run the story as it is recorded in Scripture through your imagination as if you were actually there.

Your time of prayer is a time when, under the guidance of the Holy Spirit, you take in the sights, sounds and events from the gospel story you will be preaching about. Your time of prayer is about you entering an event from the story of Jesus as recorded in Scripture. From start to finish. Once you have prayed the story in this way, you complete your prayer with a very personal time with Jesus.

6. A Conversation to Have (Colloquy)

By now you would have seen, heard and experienced a lot. Time to tell a friend all about it, wouldn't you say? We finish this time of Ignatian Gospel Contemplation by talking to Jesus as "one friend to another." As you prayed you will have had thoughts and feelings about what you have experienced. You will have new insights, new questions, new passion and new vision. I once led a small group of people through this kind of prayer. The gospel story we prayed through was Jesus cleansing the temple. There was a young woman in the group who imagined herself as one of the people with a table in the temple, selling things to the worshippers. When Jesus came in and overturned tables and scattered everything around (including her table), she became very angry. She came to me afterwards to talk it through because she realized that her anger was not right. The time of prayer had exposed an area in her life that she did not want Jesus to touch and have lordship over. This time of talking with Jesus "as one friend to another" is a time when you tell him how you are honestly feeling and what you are honestly thinking –

especially if it is a time when you are feeling strong emotions like anger or sadness, or strong thoughts such as a new idea or a strong memory. So much can come out of this conversation with Jesus. It may be that you come to a deeper place of commitment to God, or a greater commitment to serve God and love others. One way to consider the time of prayer is that you have loved the Lord your God with all your heart, soul and mind. Now the time talking with Jesus is focused on loving your neighbour as yourself (Matt 22:37–39). Or, in other words, how will your life change because of this prayer you have just experienced? The answers to such questions and this time of talking with Jesus as one friend to another prepare you for the sermon you will write as a result of this time of prayer.

This time of prayer using Ignatian Gospel Contemplation is when you listen to the story.

We can say that you begin the time of prayer having lived a story, you then listen to the story through praying the Scriptures, and now you are empowered to tell the story in a new way.

Just like *lectio divina*, Ignatian Gospel Contemplation helps us listen to the story of Jesus. We become like the disciples on the road to Emmaus as they listened to Jesus talking about how he fulfils Scripture.

We listen to his story.

After we have listened carefully, we are like those same disciples returning to Jerusalem full of the good news of Jesus Christ.

We have a story to tell.

Remember our approach in this book: in life, all of us are *living* a story, *listening* to a story and *telling* a story. Often we do not even think about it because the story we live, listen to and tell is what we do from the moment we wake up every day. Our living, listening and telling is what makes up our very life. We all are living lives that are in need of the in-breaking message and Word of Christ. So the starting point is lives which are a mixture of faithfulness and faithlessness to God. The story we live is in constant need of "listening to the story of Christ" so that the "story we tell" changes and therefore the "story we live" changes.

The story of the road to Emmaus shows us disciples living a story (walking in sadness having not understood the story of Jesus), listening to a story (as Jesus begins with "Moses and the Prophets" and shows how he fulfils Scripture), and telling a story (as the disciples return to Jerusalem with the good news of the resurrection).

Let's now follow the process of writing an actual sermon by using *lectio divina* and Ignatian Gospel Contemplation. In the next two chapters I will take you through the process and you can watch over my shoulder while I pray the passage of Scripture and write a sermon outline.

Questions for Life

Choose a Bible passage and pray using Ignatian Gospel Contemplation. What did you find easy about listening to the story? What did you find difficult about listening to the story?

5

Listening Using *Lectio Divina*
Preparing the Sermon –
1 Chronicles 22:17–19

Preparatory Prayer

I begin my time of prayer being mindful of all the tasks that await me after I have finished praying. This is a pressure. Then there are the noises outside the room where I am praying. This is a distraction. Yet I begin to focus on the task of praying the Scripture before me. All the busyness, the tasks that need to be done today and tomorrow, the distracting noises outside – all these can wait. This time of prayer is for real and for now. And so I ask God to quieten my mind and soul. I ask for grace so that I may give myself to God. I begin to feel the effect of God answering my prayer.

Lectio (Read Aloud)

I turn to the passage of Scripture I will be praying and preaching on. For the purposes of this chapter, I asked my wife to choose the passage. I do not want to choose one of my favourite passages or a passage that I think will be easy to preach from. By asking my wife to choose, I am committing myself to engage with a text regardless of what it is. I want to show you that the discipline of preaching includes preaching on passages of Scripture which might be new to you or difficult for you. Yet, we must still preach from them. If you are in a church which follows a lectionary, you will be required to preach from passages that you would not have chosen for yourself. Or if you are preaching a series through a book of the Bible, you will come across parts of Scripture which you might be tempted not to preach from. However, good expository preaching involves preaching the whole counsel of God (Acts 20:27).

The passage my wife chose is 1 Chronicles 22:17–19. I am not familiar with it.

1 Chronicles 22:17–19

Then David ordered all the leaders of Israel to help his son Solomon. [18] He said to them, "Is not the Lord your God with you? And has he not granted you rest on every side? For he has given the inhabitants of the land into my hands, and the land is subject to the Lord and to his people. [19] Now devote your heart and soul to seeking the Lord your God. Begin to build the sanctuary of the Lord God, so that you may bring the ark of the covenant of the Lord and the sacred articles belonging to God into the temple that will be built for the name of the Lord."

I begin my *lectio*: I read the passage aloud six times. As I read I am listening carefully to hear whether a particular word, phrase or sentence draws my attention. On the first reading I note one sentence. However I want to be sure this is the part of the reading the Spirit is bringing to my attention. So I read the passage another five times. When you read and pray a passage of Scripture in this way, you will decide how many times to read the text. Sometimes it will be more and other times less. There is no set rule.

The part of 1 Chronicles 22:17–19 that takes my attention is in verse 19: "Now devote your heart and soul to seeking the Lord your God." Even though this part of the prayer, *lectio*, is simply the time to read the text, I discover I am thinking about all that is happening in these verses. I realize that I might be beginning to move into the next part of the prayer: *meditatio*. I do not try too hard to stop these thoughts. When using *lectio divina*, any one of the four parts (*lectio, meditatio, oratio, contemplatio*) can begin to happen at any point. I remember that I am praying to God and by the Spirit of God anything can happen at any time. So I do not attempt to control this time. I am talking with God about the passage of Scripture and God is talking with me.

The kinds of things that are coming to mind are varied.

I think about the fact that Solomon is the son of David and Bathsheba. I recall the terrible events that led up to the birth of Solomon (2 Sam 11–12:25). I then think about how these words in 1 Chronicles 22 describe the rest that the Lord has given to Israel. I think about how the land and inhabitants are subject to the Lord. I ponder briefly on the ark of the covenant and the sacred articles all being intended for a great place of worship for the name of the Lord. In all of this though, the words of verse 19 still stand out for me:

"Now devote your heart and soul to seeking the Lord your God."

Meditatio (Think Deeply)

I now deliberately begin to think deeply about why the words of verse 19 are the words I am drawn to.

To start with, I think about the pattern and shape of the story before verse 19.

Verse 18 talks about the activity of God in bringing rest to the nation of Israel. It is as if God has prepared the way for the people so that they can devote themselves to seeking God (v. 19). I think about the story of Israel being prepared: the Exodus and God bringing Israel to the Promised Land.

My thoughts are racing. Different things are quickly coming to mind and they do not seem to be in any kind of order.

I was thinking about the Exodus, and now suddenly I think about John the Baptist preparing the way for Jesus (Mark 1:1–8).

Next moment I think of Romans 5:8: "But God demonstrates his own love for us in this: While we were still sinners, Christ died for us." I think about how that is an example of God preparing the way so that people can have rest and devote themselves to seeking God.

Maybe all these thoughts are linked by the common thought of God preparing the way for people to encounter him.

Then I think about the temple at the end of verse 19 and Solomon building the temple. My mind goes to John 2 when Jesus refers to himself as the temple.

I remember another verse about God preparing the way: "we love because he first loved us" (1 John 4:19). This verse comes to mind because of the description in 1 Chronicles 22:18 of God's giving peace and rest and how that leads to the call to be devoted to seeking God (v. 19). I think about how God's grace gives me the opportunity to seek, know and love him (vv. 17–18). I also note that after the words of verse 19 and the call to be devoted to seeking the "Lord your God," there is the call to bring sacred articles to God (v. 19b–c).

As you can see, I am having lots of thoughts and they might even seem muddled. I am not worried about this. I know that God is with me and that

I am praying the Scriptures. I trust that God will help me and that the most important thoughts will become clear.

I begin to focus on one question especially: "Why does verse 19 call to me?"

In this very moment I begin to feel emotional. Even though I have been thinking about Israel's history leading up to 1 Chronicles 22 and the ministry of Jesus later in Scripture, I have been *thinking*. That is an important part of *meditatio* but suddenly I am *feeling* something. I realize that the words of verse 19 touch a longing in my heart. The words, "Now devote your heart and soul to seeking the Lord your God," touch places in my heart and times in my life when I have lost my first love for Jesus (Rev 2:4). These are memories of when I have failed to be devoted to God and have not sought him.

I meditate about how God prepares a way and how I might respond to God. I am challenged that there are times of busyness in my life when such spirituality (being aware of God's preparing a way in life) and service (responding to God) have not had these words at their heart:

"Now devote your heart and soul to seeking the Lord your God."

The words before verse 19a describe spirituality: God is with Israel (v. 18).

The words after verse 19a describe service: building the temple and filling it (v. 19b–c).

Is it possible to claim to be spiritual and serve God and not be devoted to God and seek him? Yes! I remember being exactly like that. I remember the feelings when I am like that. This is why I am feeling emotional. I remember those times and realize I can still be like that: believing I am spiritual and serving but not being devoted to seeking the Lord my God. Scripture is challenging me.

"Why does verse 19 call to me?" For me, this verse is a call to return home. I think of the great theologian of centuries ago, Augustine, who wrote "the Bible is a letter from home." These few words from 1 Chronicles 22, which are thousands of years old, are speaking to me today. This is the wonder of the presence of God and the power of the Bible. I am being called home. I am being called to draw near to God. I am being called to devote myself to seeking the Lord my God.

I find myself thinking of the prodigal son (Luke 15:11–32). I think about the moment when the prodigal son "comes to his senses" (Luke 15:17). Before that moment a lot had happened, and after that moment a lot happens. Yet when he comes to his senses he decides to return to his father. His heart and mind are drawing him back home. This moment seems to illustrate the words "Now devote your heart and soul to seeking the Lord your God." The prodigal expects to return home to become a slave. Yet the father has other ideas and it becomes a time of celebration, reconciliation and fellowship. As I think during this time of *mediatio*, I wonder whether there is some kind of connection between 1 Chronicles 22:17–19 and the story of the prodigal son. I wonder whether the connection is that both have at their heart the call to "devote your heart and soul to seeking the Lord your God." After all, King David knew what it was like to be a prodigal son. The very mention of his son Solomon in 1 Chronicles 22:17 reminds us that David had sinned against God by committing adultery with Bathsheba and murdering her husband Uriah.

"Now devote your heart and soul to seeking the Lord your God." Here is the quiet place. Here is the meaning of life. Again words of Augustine come to mind: "My soul is restless until it finds rest in you." By devoting my heart and soul to seeking the Lord my God I find rest. Like David. Like the prodigal son. Like the nation of Israel.

I think about how this message from 1 Chronicles 22 is saying "Wherever you are, wherever anyone is, God has done something and God is yet to do something. And nestled in that is the call to 'devote your heart and soul to seeking the Lord your God.'"

Oratio (Pray Honestly)

As this part of the prayer comes to an end, a prayer naturally begins to form. I pray:

> "Lord Jesus, help me to see you in the midst of all that is happening. Help me to see what you have done and what you are doing. Help me to be devoted in seeking you with all my heart and soul – so that my restless soul will find rest in you."

Contemplatio (Rest Quietly)

The last part of *lectio divina* invites me to simply rest in God. To begin to still my heart and mind. To gaze at Jesus as he gazes at me. The fact that the passage I have been praying speaks of rest and also the mention of the temple pointing to a place of lasting, eternal and worshipful rest both help this time of *contemplatio*.

The words that have struck me, "Now devote your heart and soul to seeking the Lord your God," are being fulfilled as I sit with God. This is a time without effort.

Then I am prompted to pray the Lord's Prayer. This I do and finish my time of *lectio divina.*

From the time I began until the end has been just under an hour.

Living a Story, Listening to a Story, Telling a Story

Now I begin studying and writing the sermon. But my study for the sermon is now coloured by the prayer experience. Think of it like this. When I first came to the passage, I had been walking on the road to Emmaus (living a story). I had tasks to do both that day and in the days to come. As I began to pray, distractions threatened to draw me away from this time. All of this was me "living a story" as I began walking on the road to Emmaus. Then, as I prayed 1 Chronicles 22:17–19 through *lectio divina,* Jesus began to speak to me and with me. When Jesus opened the Scriptures for the two disciples on the road to Emmaus in Luke 24, they were better able to understand him and the plan of God. So it is when you and I pray the Scriptures using this ancient way of praying. This is the time when the preacher "listens to a story." I now begin to prepare the sermon on 1 Chronicles 22:17–19. I am "telling a story." The two on the road to Emmaus returned to Jerusalem to tell the others "We have seen the Lord," and the sermon birthed out of prayer and preparation will have the same message. You too will stand before your people and say "I have seen the Lord!"

Sermon Outline

During my prayer, I had a lot of thoughts and considered other places in Scripture which came to mind. I am also aware that a lot of my prayer focused on *my* relationship with God, and yet the passage in 1 Chronicles 22 focuses on a *nation's* relationship with God. I realize that, as I continue to study this passage and place it in its historical context, I will need to study it as a message to a community of faith and not just to individuals. Yet, this passage is also a message from a single leader (David) to other leaders (of Israel) about an individual (Solomon). I am comfortable with the personal approach I have taken during prayer because, at one level, we all need to respond to God as individuals. However, if the final form of my sermon stays only at the level of the individual, I will not have preached the true burden of the text. So I am careful to make sure that I study the passage with both of these aspects in mind.

The words of the Scripture passage are alive in my heart. The challenge to devote one's self to seeking the Lord God will be at the heart of the sermon. The words from 1 Chronicles 22 which I focused on during *lectio divina* appear in the middle of the verses 17–19. I notice a shape to this passage of Scripture, and I begin to organize an initial sermon outline around the actual verses:

1. What needed to happen before: God prepared a home (vv. 17–18)

> *Then David ordered all the leaders of Israel to help his son Solomon. He said to them, "Is not the Lord your God with you? And has he not granted you rest on every side? For he has given the inhabitants of the land into my hands, and the land is subject to the Lord and to his people."*

2. What needs to happen now: we turn towards home (v. 19a)

> *Now devote your heart and soul to seeking the Lord your God.*

3. What needs to happen next: God inhabits home (v. 19b–c)

> *Begin to build the sanctuary of the Lord God, so that you may bring the ark of the covenant of the Lord and the sacred articles belonging to God into the temple that will be built for the name of the Lord.*

I look at this outline and something does not seem quite right. However, the effect of *lectio divina* is still with me. It is now several hours since I prayed yet the experience is still very much in my heart and mind. You will experience this too. The time of prayer is like a plant taking root in your life. Many centuries ago, the Benedictine monks would pray using *lectio divina*. They would read and pray and work. So even after they had listened to Scripture and prayed about a passage using *lectio divina*, they would continue to pray while doing their daily tasks. The Word would continue to speak. I discover the same thing happening to me as I continue in my other work and activities for the day. I continue to wrestle with the insight of devoting my heart and soul to seeking the Lord my God (v. 19). I prayed this Scripture for one hour at 7:30 a.m. Nearly twelve hours later, when I was doing something entirely different, new thoughts came to my mind. *Lectio divina* had not stopped its work in my heart.

I think more about how 1 Chronicles 22:17–19 is a message from an old leader (David) to current leaders (of Israel) about a young leader (Solomon). This is important for me to remember. Some of my earlier reflection had made connections with the story of the prodigal son (Luke 15:11–32). The three parables in Luke 15 are told by a leader (Jesus) to leaders (Pharisees and teachers of the law). I begin to realize that, for this sermon to be true to the text, it will need to be a message for leaders.

Suddenly it comes to me that the words from 1 Chronicles 22 can be captured in three words. These three words are the three great treasures of Israel as the people of God: land, law and temple:

1. **Land** (v. 18): David speaks of God granting peace and giving the land to Israel.

2. **Law** (v. 19a): David calls the leaders to devote themselves to seeking God. This means to love God with all one's being. Jesus said the greatest commandment was to love God with all your heart, mind, soul and strength.

3. **Temple** (v. 19b–c): David speaks of building the temple and bringing the ark of covenant and sacred articles into the temple.

The shape of the sermon is slowly changing. The words of being devoted to seeking God are still at the heart of what I will preach about. Yet for the sermon to be true to the text, it will need to be with leaders in mind and it will need to respect the three great pillars of the Hebrew faith. I also notice that the title "Lord God" appears in each of the three parts of this passage. So this is a message for leaders drawing their attention to the presence of the Lord God through three gifts from God: land, law and temple.

My sermon outline now looks like this:

Leaders for Life
1 Chronicles 22:17–19

1. A Land to Live In: God Is Present (vv. 17–18)

In this part of the sermon, I will briefly explain the journey of Israel from slavery in Egypt to their new home in the promised land. This part of 1 Chronicles 22 summarizes the goodness of God in giving the nation peace during the reign of King David. The point is made that this is all done by and for the Lord God. This part of the sermon will challenge leaders about how they view the goodness of God in the places they live and the people they lead. Do they remember where they have come from? Do they recall the ways the Lord God has led them and their people? Have they made the mistake of hoarding the goodness of God and forgetting that it is all from the Lord God and everything is his? Have they become blind and deaf to the many things that show that God is present? It is easy to forget all this during times of peace and blessing. Israel often made this mistake as they lived in the land. In what ways do leaders of the church of Jesus Christ make the same mistake? These are the kinds of issues I will work on in this part of the sermon.

I will also use the parable of the prodigal son as a careful illustration. The prodigal son lived on his father's land but became blind to the goodness and kindness of his father. He left his father's home in the most offensive way. The prodigal son lived in the land and did not respect his father's presence.

This first sermon point is energized by the challenge I have felt to devote my heart and soul to seeking the Lord my God. I can see in David's words in these opening verses that it can be easy to forget that all I have is from the Lord God and for the Lord God. If I am not careful, it is easy to forget that God is present in the place I live and work. These mistakes can happen if we falter in our devotion to seeking God.

2. A Law to Live By: God Is Waiting (v. 19a)

Now I come to the part of the passage that gripped me during *lectio divina*. Here I will explain the nature of the law of Moses and the way Jesus summed it up: love God and love your neighbour. I may need to talk about how, as Christians, we view the Old Testament law as a bad thing but that, at its heart, it was about helping the people of God know and love God. These words at the beginning of verse 19 are one way of summing up the law and of God's hopes for all of humanity: to know and love the Lord our God.

These words are challenging. They are confronting. Can we say "yes Lord" in response to them? Here I can draw on the next part of the Parable of the Prodigal Son. When feeding the pigs, his heart and soul turn towards home and he now seeks his father. This is a helpful illustration for this part of 1 Chronicles 22. The prodigal son's father waits for the return of his son. Here in my second point of this sermon. I will try and show that this is a good law to live by: God is waiting. Devote your heart and soul to seeking the Lord your God. Surely this is the true heart of leadership: what leaders devote themselves to. What can be more important for a leader of God's people than to seek the Lord our God?

3. A Lord to Live For: God Is Worshipped (v. 19b–c)

The third point of the sermon will explain the nature of the temple that Solomon built for the Lord God. I will need to talk about what the sanctuary, the ark of the covenant and the sacred articles are. I will make the point that, just like the land (point 1) and our lives (point 2), everything mentioned in verse 19b–c belongs to the Lord God. This is a very important point in our understanding of God and all of life. This is all leading to "building" lives which are directed to the worship of God. Even our mission to those who do not know God is so that people may live life at its best by worshipping the Lord God. Good leadership helps people to bring all things to God in worship, understanding that all things belong to the Lord our God anyway.

Again the story of the prodigal son helps me here. I will need to be careful not to make this sermon appear to be a sermon on Luke 15. I will keep my comments brief in the sermon so that the story of the prodigal son serves as an illustration only. At the end of that story the prodigal is welcomed back with great celebration. However, the elder brother is angry that his brother is being treated so well by their father. Then the father makes an amazing statement which has echoes about all things belonging to God: "'My son' the father said, 'you are always with me *and everything I have* is yours'" (Luke 15:31). While all things are God's, in his kindness and grace he mysteriously gives them to us. In seeking God, we discover he is waiting for us and we discover some of the depths of his generosity and kindness.

I still have a lot of work to finish the sermon. However, I know when I preach this sermon I will be "telling a story" in a new way. My life has been energized through *lectio divina* and I have been challenged by the Spirit about my devotion to seeking God. This will come through in my sermon even though I may not actually describe to the listeners what happened during my prayer time.

"Lord Jesus, help us to see you in the midst of all that is happening. Help us to see what you have done and what you are doing. Help us to be devoted in seeking you with all our hearts and souls – so that our restless souls will find rest in you."

Questions for Life

As you read this chapter, what thoughts came to your mind about the Bible passage? What part of this story is God inviting you to listen to?

6

Listening Using Ignatian Gospel Contemplation
Preparing the Sermon – John 1:43–51

1. Prayer to Start (Preparatory Prayer)

I begin my time of prayer. What is my very first thought? I remember an email I was meant to send but had forgotten. Here I am beginning to pray and my first thought has nothing to do with prayer. However, I understand that distracting thoughts and events can easily happen during prayer. I do not worry about it. I write myself a note to remind myself to send the email later and I return to prayer.

I am still and quiet. I do not say anything to begin with. I simply sit with God and my heart and mind begin to think about God.

In the stillness I am expectant about what I am about to do: pray about an event from the Gospels. I am excited and I am looking forward to it. As I remain quiet I become aware of the love of God. I realize that God's love is always there, but in my busyness I may not be quiet enough or attentive enough to really notice it. However, in this moment I do sense the love of God. In fact, for some reason, I am particularly aware of God's kindness. I have the sense that God has shown kindness to me recently. This thought and thanksgiving bubbles to the surface during this prayer.

As I pray and prepare to engage with Scripture I am also aware that sometimes my own imagination and thoughts are not reliable. Part of what I pray at this time is acknowledging that, while I do not trust myself, I will entrust myself to God's grace.

As I begin to draw this opening part of Ignatian Gospel Contemplation to an end, I find there is a sense of rest and quietness within me. I now begin the second part of this prayer: reading the Scriptures.

2. A Story to Read (1st Prelude – Subject Matter)

The story I chose to pray and to preach on is John 1:43–51. It is the story of Nathanael meeting Jesus.

John 1:43–51

[43] The next day Jesus decided to leave for Galilee. Finding Philip, he said to him, "Follow me."

[44] Philip, like Andrew and Peter, was from the town of Bethsaida. [45] Philip found Nathanael and told him, "We have found the one Moses wrote about in the Law, and about whom the prophets also wrote – Jesus of Nazareth, the son of Joseph."

[46] "Nazareth! Can anything good come from there?" Nathanael asked.

"Come and see," said Philip.

[47] When Jesus saw Nathanael approaching, he said of him, "Here truly is an Israelite in whom there is no deceit."

[48] "How do you know me?" Nathanael asked.

Jesus answered, "I saw you while you were still under the fig tree before Philip called you."

[49] Then Nathanael declared, "Rabbi, you are the Son of God; you are the king of Israel."

[50] Jesus said, "You believe because I told you I saw you under the fig tree. You will see greater things than that." [51] He then added, "Very truly I tell you, you will see 'heaven open, and the angels of God ascending and descending on' the Son of Man."

I read the passage slowly and aloud four times. My main purpose is to read and listen to the story. Even though I will think and reflect on the story later in the prayer time, I notice that my mind begins to connect parts of the story as I read it. I do not try and stop those thoughts and neither do I try to really study the story at this time. For example, I am struck by the different declarations Jesus and Nathanael make about each other (vv. 47 and 49). I am particularly struck by all the titles for Jesus used by Nathanael ("Rabbi," "Son of God" and "King of Israel"). However, at this point in the prayer my main task is simply to read the story. I want to become familiar with the story so that later I can picture it and imagine it.

After the fourth reading, I decide I am ready to go to the next stage of the prayer. Sometimes I will read the Bible passage more times, sometimes fewer times. There is no set rule. You will know when you are familiar enough with the reading to go on to the next part of the prayer.

3. A Place to Imagine (2nd Prelude – Composition of Place)

I close my eyes and begin to imagine what the scene in John 1:43–51 might look like. The passage gives very few details about the scenery. Actually, there is only one detail about the place where this event happened: a fig tree. And I am not even very sure what a fig tree looks like. Nevertheless, I begin to picture the scene. How I picture the scene is not as important as what happens in the scene. As long as I faithfully recall the events and conversations described in John 1:43–51, other details simply paint the picture. Unless there is something about the scene that is particularly described, my imagination can create the scene as best I am able.

In my mind's eye I see it is a sunny day in a place where there are low hills, covered with grass. A dusty road winds through the hills. A little way off there is a gnarly tree, its trunk twisted with age. The branches spread out and cast a shadow on the ground around the tree. There is someone sitting in the shade, leaning against the trunk of the tree. However, he is too far away for me to make out his physical features. Jesus and Philip are standing close to where I am and I can see them clearly. There are a few other people around too.

This is the scene I imagine from reading the account in John's Gospel. The scene is true-to-life but obviously not exactly as it was. No one today knows what it really looked like; the main task is simply to make it realistic.

At this stage of my prayer the action in the story as described in John 1 has not commenced. This is important. The scene is set but the action is yet to begin. That will happen soon. The next part of the prayer is very important. I do not want to rush this next part.

4. A Grace to Desire (3rd Prelude – Asking for Desired Grace)

I now prayerfully consider what grace I hope to experience as I continue in prayerful engagement with this story about Nathanael meeting Jesus. The desire for a particular experience has slowly become clearer as I have gone through the previous steps. Through quietening myself, reading the Bible passage several times and imagining the scene, I realize that I desire grace to know Jesus sees me and that I may be drawn to him to know and follow him.

Just like Nathanael.

So I pray:

> Lord, grant me the grace to really know in my heart that you see me. Draw me to yourself so I may know you and follow you.

5.   An Event to Experience (Gospel Contemplation)

Now I close my eyes again. This helps me concentrate to pray the scene from John 1:43–51 in my imagination. You might be able to concentrate in a different way. That's ok. The important thing is to be comfortable and to concentrate so you can focus on the Bible story you are imagining.

I have chosen not to imagine myself as one of the characters in the story. Instead I imagine I am in the scene but standing off to one side, watching the events happen and listening to what is said.

I "see" Jesus approach Philip, who is standing with some other people. Jesus says to Philip, "Follow me" (v. 43). Philip looks at the others he is standing with. He seems surprised at Jesus' words. However, he leaves the small group he is with and begins to walk with Jesus on the dusty road that winds through and past the low grassy hills. And there in the distance is the old twisted fig tree with someone sitting in its shade. The person is relaxing and leaning back against the light coloured, aged trunk.

Philip begins to walk towards the fig tree and Jesus waits on the road. I follow Philip as he approaches the person whose name I know is Nathanael.

Philip says to Nathanael, "We have found the one Moses wrote about in the Law, and about whom the prophets also wrote . . ." (v. 45).

At these words I can see Nathanael's face brighten with expectation and great interest. He leans forward listening carefully to what his friend is saying.

Philip continues, "Jesus of Nazareth, the son of Joseph" (v. 45).

Nathanael flops back against the tree. He is smiling. The excited look on his face is now replaced by amusement. He really thinks this is a joke.

"Nazareth!" he exclaims smiling. "Can anything good come from there?" (v. 46).

Philip replies, "Come and see" (v. 46).

Nathanael looks unconvinced and sceptical. He slowly pushes himself to his feet. Obviously he would rather stay under his tree than meet this Nazarene.

He and Philip walk slowly across the grass towards the dusty road where Jesus is waiting. As Nathanael comes closer, Jesus smiles and says to him, "Here truly is an Israelite in whom there is no deceit" (v. 47).

For some reason when Jesus says this, my mind goes to another moment earlier in John 1. I hear John the Baptist making *his* declaration when he saw Jesus, "Look, the Lamb of God who takes away the sin of the world!" (v. 29). This moment is not part of the Nathanael story, but for some reason I remember it as Jesus speaks to Nathanael. Even though I am still in the scene of Nathanael's story, I am hearing echoes of other declarations scattered through the stories of John 1.

My attention returns to what is happening between Jesus and Nathanael. I realize that Jesus' words have made a deep impact on Nathanael. For some reason, I am feeling something very deeply as I hear the words Jesus spoke to this Israelite:

"Here truly is an Israelite in whom there is no deceit."

There is stillness in this moment. Nathanael's casual and disbelieving manner is suddenly changed. The relaxed and playful look on his face changes and he becomes solemn and serious. In this moment in the prayer, I am feeling something deeply. My emotions are in play. I am drawn into this drama. I do not fully understand why Jesus said what he did but I feel something deeply. Somehow Jesus has touched Nathanael's heart. Somehow Jesus has spoken life-giving and life-changing words. Somehow there are a lot of unspoken things happening. Obviously the text does not give details about what was going on in Nathanael's heart, yet in the place of prayer I am left with the impression that there is an unspoken conversation happening. Nathanael's deep hopes and dreams are being fulfilled in Jesus. Israel's deep hopes and dreams are being fulfilled in Jesus. Something is happening that is significant, personal and somehow linked to the call on Israel as the people of God.

And somehow in the time of this prayer, this part of the story is affecting me as I watch on.

"How do you know me?" (v. 48) replies an astonished Nathanael.

"I saw you while you were still under the fig tree before Philip called you" (v. 48), Jesus answers.

Then Nathanael declares, "Rabbi, you are the Son of God; you are the king of Israel" (v. 49). I am struck by the richness of Nathanael's words. Here his hopes are put into words and his hope is placed in Christ.

Jesus answers, "You believe because I told you I saw you under the fig tree. You will see greater things than that. Very truly I tell you, you will see 'heaven open, and the angels of God ascending and descending on' the Son of Man" (vv. 50–51).

This part of the prayer comes to an end.

Even though I have prayerfully imagined the scene and followed the events and conversations faithfully, at this point I cannot testify to any great revelation. That is ok. The most important thing is that I have immersed myself in the Scripture through this way of praying. I trust the Spirit will continue to guide me as I begin the final step of this way of prayer.

6. A Conversation to Have (Colloquy)

I now begin to talk with Jesus as "one friend to another" about what I have just experienced. There is a lot to talk about.

I talk to Jesus about how, in this story in John 1:43–51, ordinary conversations lead to amazing statements. For example, "Follow me" (v. 43) leads to "We have found the one Moses wrote about in the Law, and about whom the prophets also wrote – Jesus of Nazareth, the son of Joseph" (v. 45). I talk to Jesus about how one sentence begins with the great names "Moses" and "the prophets" and ends with a new and unexpected name: "Jesus of Nazareth, son of Joseph."

I talk with Jesus about another ordinary conversation in the story that leads to an amazing statement. I talk about how Nathanael says, "Nazareth! Can anything good come from there?" which leads to the response "Come and see" (v. 46), which leads to Nathanael declaring that Jesus is the "Son of God and the King of Israel" (v. 49).

I talk to Jesus about how the conversations in this story seem to have gaps. It is as if one person is trying to show the less serious person new life and new vision.

- Nathanael's joke about Nazareth (v. 46) is responded to by Philip's invitation to come and see (v. 46).
- Nathanael's joke about Jesus of Nazareth (v. 46) is responded to by Jesus' declaration that Nathanael is a true Israelite in whom there is not deceit (v. 47).

- Nathanael's question about how does Jesus know him (v. 48) is answered by Jesus saying he saw Nathanael before Philip even spoke to him (v. 48).
- Nathanael's wonderful declaration of faith (v. 49) is greeted by Jesus promising to all present that they will see even greater things (vv. 50–51).

I talk to Jesus about all these back-and-forth conversations. They seem scattered, but as I talk to Jesus about them I begin to understand that the conversations are focused and centred on him. I begin to realize that the more the conversations continue, the closer the people in the story draw to Jesus. I slowly see that hopes were in the hearts of the people, but that maybe hope was beginning to leak out of their lives before they met Jesus.

In this part of the prayer, I also talk with Jesus about how I was captivated by all the strong echoes from the Old Testament:

- Moses and the prophets (v. 45)
- The title "Israelite" (v. 47)
- The significance of fig trees as a symbol and emblem of Israel (vv. 48 and 50)
- The title "king of Israel" (v. 49)
- That to sit under a fig tree (and a vine for that matter) is often a sign of God's blessing of peace and rest (vv. 48 and 50)
- "Angels ascending and descending" is a reference to Jacob's dream of a stairway to heaven at Bethel (Gen 28).

The effect of this is the realization that ordinary conversations and events can lead to extraordinary conversations and events. I talk with Jesus about how maybe, like Nathanael, I am sitting under a fig tree and thinking that everything is ordinary and normal. I sit there thinking I am living my life, yet I am surrounded by symbols, conversations and events that point me to God's story. I think about the fact that I am living *in* God's story and I sometimes make the mistake of thinking I am living in *my* story.

The more I talk with Jesus, the more this thought grows. Instead of Nathanael sitting under that fig tree I see *me* sitting under that fig tree. I sit there with hopes of God, but my conversation does not always reflect that hope. Maybe it's time for me to get to my feet and encounter Jesus in a new way. Maybe in my conversations with others there is more of Jesus than I realize. I am challenged by the thought of being seen by Jesus and being drawn nearer to him through conversations and events. I am challenged by the thought that Jesus sees me. I am challenged by the thought that I love because he first sees me and he first loves me (1 John 4:19). I am challenged that Jesus calls me and calls us all to see and experience greater things in him. I love the way the story plays with the word "seeing" – Philip invites Nathanael to "come and see" (v. 46), then Jesus sees Nathanael (v. 48) and invites Nathanael and the others present to see greater things (v. 51).

And so finishes my praying through John 1:43–51. However the wonderful thing is that even though I have finished praying, the praying has not finished with me. I discover that the images, thoughts and challenges remain with me and continue speaking to me. So the prayer does not really end.

Living a Story, Listening to a Story, Telling a Story

Now I begin studying and writing the sermon. But my study for the sermon is now coloured by the prayer experience. Think of it like this. At the very beginning of the time of prayer I had been walking on the road to Emmaus (living a story). On this particular day I had jobs to do and people to see. Even as I began to pray I remembered I had not sent an email. All of this was me "living a story" as I began walking on the road to Emmaus. Then by praying John 1:43–51 through Ignatian Gospel Contemplation, Jesus began to speak to me and with me. Just as when Jesus opened the Scriptures for the two disciples on the road to Emmaus in Luke 24 so that they were better able to understand Jesus and the plan of God, so it is when you and I pray the Scriptures using this ancient way of praying. This is the time when the preacher "listens to a story." And after praying the passage using Ignatian Gospel Contemplation, my heart is burning and I now begin to prepare the sermon on John 1:43–51. I am "telling a story." The two on the road to Emmaus returned to Jerusalem to tell the others "We have seen the Lord," and the sermon that is birthed out of prayer and preparation will have the same message. You too will stand before your people and say "I have seen the Lord!"

Sermon Outline

Now as I begin to study the text in other ways, I begin from the experience and observations from my time of prayer. I especially remember my prayer for a grace to desire:

> "Lord, grant me the grace to really know in my heart that you see me. Draw me to yourself so I may know you and follow you."

Through my time of prayer I have experienced something of this grace, the sense of being seen by Christ but, more importantly, I have sensed how he opens our eyes and hearts to see and perceive him.

I begin collecting my observations and prayer experience in an initial sermon outline. I particularly draw on the word-play on the word "see" that is present in the story. I need to continue to work on the outline as it is a little too wordy. However, it begins to reflect some of the experience and insights I came to during my time of prayer. This outline will be tested and changed as I begin to study the text, looking closely at the story in other ways, but for now this is what I have come to:[1]

Before Our Very Eyes
John 1:43-51

Do we see Christ in Scripture? (vv. 43–45)

This part of the sermon will explore Philip's claim and experience of Jesus fulfilling the Hebrew Scriptures.

Do we see Jesus in life? (v. 46)

This part of the sermon will focus on how we can dismiss aspects of life as not being connected to God, as Nathanael dismissed Nazareth for example.

---

1. When preaching from a story in the Bible I prefer that the sermon outline is shaped by the story so that the feel and sense of the story is honoured. Sometimes when a Bible story is preached using main points (like my draft outline here) it can take away the sense of story. However, because this book is written for preachers who are beginning their ministry, I wanted to show that structure is important in a sermon. For this reason I have included this draft sermon outline using four main points.

What does Jesus see in us? (vv. 47–48)

This part of the sermon will concentrate on how Jesus sees the heart of who we are, as he saw Nathanael's heart.

What does Christ promise we will see in him? (vv. 49–51)

This part of the sermon will gather up the story and show how, through Scripture, each of us is invited to see and join the plan of God in Christ. As Jesus promises in verse 51, they will see heaven open.

I have seen how I have been living my story, I have been blessed to listen to Jesus' story, and I am energized to tell his story.

Questions for Life

As you read this chapter, what was it about the story of Nathanael that spoke to you? Listen to his story carefully.

7

The Road to Emmaus: Where Does It Lead?

L iving, listening, telling.
We have seen how these rhythms shape our lives. We have seen that of these three rhythms, listening is especially important for preachers. The story we listen to will greatly influence how we live and what we tell. This is why listening to Scripture is so important.

The focus of this book is on how to listen to God as you study the Scriptures when you prepare your sermon. When you hear what God wants to say through your sermon, everything changes. The way you preach changes. What you say when you preach changes. The people listening to your sermon change. If you meet and hear God during your sermon preparation, when you stand before your people, you will be able to say, "I have seen the Lord!" By the end of the sermon, the people will respond, "As have we!" If you know what God is saying to you as a preacher, when you preach you will not just deliver a sermon, you will be living the sermon.

We have used the story of the road to Emmaus (Luke 24:13–35) as a way of illustrating how preachers live the story, listen to the story and tell the story. We have also learnt about two ways of praying the Scriptures so we can listen closely to God's story: *lectio divina* and Ignatian Gospel Contemplation. I have given two examples of praying the Scriptures using each type of prayer and demonstrated how this can lead to a sermon outline. In this last chapter, I want us to walk the road to Emmaus again.

The two disciples in that story changed because of Jesus walking with them, opening the Scriptures and breaking bread. The story of the road to Emmaus is a story about two people being born anew. What I love about the story is that it happens in an ordinary way (two people walking on a road) but also in an extraordinary way (the victorious Christ walking and talking with them). I love that the story of the road to Emmaus involves things that are not too hard to imagine or relate to today. On the road to Emmaus we are surrounded by wonderful biblical images. The story involves a city (Jerusalem), a village (Emmaus), a road, people (those on the road, those described as having gone to the empty tomb, and the Eleven), Bible characters and the Scriptures (angels, Moses and the prophets), God's plan ("Did not the Messiah have to suffer these things and then enter his glory?"), a table and bread (Jesus sitting with the two disciples and breaking bread), and feelings and revelation (the two looked sad *and* their hearts were aflame with excitement). Encounters with Jesus, place names, people's names, spirituality, divine plans, emotion, revelation, excitement. Stand there on that road and take it all in. Stand there on that road as you live the story and desire to tell the story. Stand there on that road and listen. Because at the heart of it all it involves disciples of Jesus *listening* – an important discipline for preachers to develop. Listening to the voice of the Spirit through the Scriptures. But if we are on the road to Emmaus listening to the story of Jesus, where does this road lead?

The reason I listed all the things that appear in the story of the road to Emmaus is because those are the kinds of places, people and spaces that the road leads to. Just as Jesus took the two disciples on a journey through Scripture, this story invites you to take a similar journey. Jesus began with Moses and the prophets and explained what was said in all the Scriptures concerning himself. The road to Emmaus leads to such places and there, if you listen carefully, you will hear the story in new ways. The Bible is full of cities, villages, roads, people, prophets, homes, food and encounters with the living God. These are all places and spaces for you to learn to listen to God's story so that you are better able to live the story and tell the story. Let me show you some of the listening places and spaces the road to Emmaus can lead to, listening places and spaces that will help you develop as a preacher of the Scriptures.

It Leads to a Person to Serve (Isaiah 42:1–9; 49:1–7; 50:4–11; 52:13–53:12)

On the road to Emmaus Jesus had to explain that, as Messiah, he needed to suffer. In the book of Isaiah there are four passages which are called the "Servant Songs." They describe a person who serves God faithfully but suffers greatly. We see the ultimate fulfilment of these songs in the person and work of Christ. These four songs describe the service, suffering and sacrifice of the Servant of the Lord. Within these four songs is a wonderful description of the relationship between the Servant and God. It is a rich storehouse for reflection, inspiration, challenge and insight. There you will find encouragement of the spirit by which to relate to people, the spirit by which to serve God and the purposes of God, the spirit by which to embrace hardship, and the spirit by which to listen to God.

The road to Emmaus leads you to such a person so you can listen to him.

It Leads to a Wall to Build (Nehemiah 8)

The city of Jerusalem features in the story of the road to Emmaus. Throughout Scripture Jerusalem is the capital city for much of God's activity and plan for the world. Of course the most major event to happen in Jerusalem is the crucifixion and resurrection of Jesus. Yet Jerusalem also reminds us of how rebellious people can be towards God and the plans of God. The people of Israel had been in exile because they had rebelled against God. Finally God called them back to Jerusalem, but when they returned home there was no wall, no city, no temple and no law. In the book of Nehemiah, as the people rebuilt the wall around Jerusalem, the Levites (led by Ezra) began to read from the Scriptures to make them clear so the people could understand. A nation's life began to be rebuilt in ways that were as real as the work on the wall itself.

> They read from the Book of the Law of God, making it clear and giving the meaning so that the people understood what was being read. (Neh 8:8)

The people listened and began to live a new story and tell a new story.

The road to Emmaus leads you to such a listening place.

It Leads to a City to Inhabit (The Book of Jeremiah)

Another example of the problem of people rebelling against God is found in the book of Jeremiah. Jeremiah is called the weeping prophet. The book of Jeremiah is the story of a prophet and preacher who had an unpopular message. Even Jeremiah didn't want to preach it. Within the book of Jeremiah you will encounter his deep reluctance and anger towards God about being required to preach the Word. You will read how Jeremiah pushed back against false prophets and the spirit of the age. Jeremiah preached faithfully as the judgement of God loomed ever nearer. Jeremiah preached in a doomed city and preached a message of hope and promise with courage and conviction.

The road to Emmaus leads you to such a listening place.

It Leads to a Field to Sow (Mark 4:1–20)

As Jesus walked on the road to Emmaus and spoke his message, he was sowing seeds in the hearts of his two travelling companions. The harvest from the seed Jesus sowed that day was wonderful. The road leads to a field to sow. One of the few parables Jesus ever explained was the Parable of the Sower. In this parable three soils describe common responses to the message of Jesus Christ. The seed (the Word of God) is sown in the lives of people and the presence of evil, persecution/hardship, and the worries, desires and cares of the world get in the way. Preachers will do well to keep these soils in mind when they preach; remembering it is to such settings they preach *into* and *from* (for such soils can describe your own heart). However, there is one soil from which an enormous and amazing harvest can emerge.

The road to Emmaus leads you to such a listening place.

It Leads to a Scroll to Read (Luke 4:18–19)

Jesus took the two on the road to Emmaus on a journey deep into Scripture. In Luke 4 we read that Jesus goes to the synagogue as was his custom and finds a passage from Isaiah he wants to read to the people. On that day he took those listeners on a journey into Scripture. He read this majestic passage:

> The Spirit of the Lord is on me,
>> because he has anointed me
>> to proclaim good news to the poor.
> He has sent me to proclaim freedom for the prisoners
>> and recovery of sight for the blind,
> to set the oppressed free,
>> to proclaim the year of the Lord's favour.

He then announces that this Scripture is fulfilled in that moment and in their hearing. Does your preaching continue to advance this good news?

The road to Emmaus leads you to such a scroll to listen to.

It Leads to a World to Engage (The Acts of the Apostles)

The road to Emmaus goes from a city, to a village, to a house, back to a city and to another house. The road led to lots of different places where the same good news was listened to and experienced. When you read the book of the Acts of the Apostles, you will see all the different situations and styles of preaching that abound in Acts. It is an exciting book to prayerfully read as you consider the wondrous events that contributed to the proclamation of the gospel. At the heart of it all is the message of the resurrection of Christ and the kingdom of God. Preaching took place in synagogues, marketplaces, houses, prisons, at river sides, philosophers' gatherings, courts of law, royal courts – and the style of preaching ranged from biblical surveys, personal testimony, powerful reasoning, heartfelt appeals, biblical interpretation, and reviews of poetry to defendant hearings in court.

The road to Emmaus leads to such a listening world.

It Leads to a Church to Lead (1 Corinthians 1:18–2:5)

The road to Emmaus had different people thinking and feeling different things. At the start of the story there was sadness, then surprise, then a rebuke, and then wonder and joy. Among the people of God on any given occasion there will be all sorts of emotions, thoughts and states of being present. We see this in Paul's First Letter to the Corinthians. In the opening passages of 1 Corinthians, Paul focuses on the message of the cross and Christ crucified. The Corinthian church was a church with problems, divisions, arguments, scandals, proud leaders, questions, worship wars, pressures from idol-worshippers, confusion about belief in Jesus, and challenges about how to best live Christ-like lives in the marketplace. Paul begins this letter by declaring his preaching programme (1 Cor 2:1–5):

> And so it was with me, brothers and sisters. When I came to you, I did not come with eloquence or human wisdom as I proclaimed to you the testimony about God. For I resolved to know nothing while I was with you except Jesus Christ and him crucified. I came to you in weakness with great fear and trembling. My message and my preaching were not with wise and persuasive words, but with a demonstration of the Spirit's power, so that your faith might not rest on human wisdom, but on God's power.

The road to Emmaus leads to such a listening place.

All of these places and spaces are the kinds of places and spaces you as a preacher will preach into. These are the kinds of places and spaces in which you will live the story of Jesus, listen to the story of Jesus, and tell the story of Jesus.

If you listen carefully to the story of Jesus in Scripture, when you stand before people in these kinds of places and spaces, you will be able to say, "I have seen the Lord!" By the end of the sermon, the people will respond, "As have we!"

Living the story.

Listening to the story.

Telling the story.

> May the God of hope fill you with all joy and peace as you trust in him, so that you may overflow with hope by the power of the Holy Spirit. (Rom 15:13)

Questions for Life

Which one of the biblical images attracted you the most? What is God saying to you about that? Listen carefully.

Langham
PARTNERSHIP

Langham Literature and its imprints are a ministry of Langham Partnership.

Langham Partnership is a global fellowship working in pursuit of the vision God entrusted to its founder John Stott –

to facilitate the growth of the church in maturity and Christ-likeness through raising the standards of biblical preaching and teaching.

Our vision is to see churches in the majority world equipped for mission and growing to maturity in Christ through the ministry of pastors and leaders who believe, teach and live by the Word of God.

Our mission is to strengthen the ministry of the Word of God through:
- nurturing national movements for biblical preaching
- fostering the creation and distribution of evangelical literature
- enhancing evangelical theological education

especially in countries where churches are under-resourced.

Our ministry

Langham Preaching partners with national leaders to nurture indigenous biblical preaching movements for pastors and lay preachers all around the world. With the support of a team of trainers from many countries, a multi-level programme of seminars provides practical training, and is followed by a programme for training local facilitators. Local preachers' groups and national and regional networks ensure continuity and ongoing development, seeking to build vigorous movements committed to Bible exposition.

Langham Literature provides majority world preachers, scholars and seminary libraries with evangelical books and electronic resources through publishing and distribution, grants and discounts. The programme also fosters the creation of indigenous evangelical books in many languages, through writer's grants, strengthening local evangelical publishing houses, and investment in major regional literature projects, such as one volume Bible commentaries like *The Africa Bible Commentary* and *The South Asia Bible Commentary*.

Langham Scholars provides financial support for evangelical doctoral students from the majority world so that, when they return home, they may train pastors and other Christian leaders with sound, biblical and theological teaching. This programme equips those who equip others. Langham Scholars also works in partnership with majority world seminaries in strengthening evangelical theological education. A growing number of Langham Scholars study in high quality doctoral programmes in the majority world itself. As well as teaching the next generation of pastors, graduated Langham Scholars exercise significant influence through their writing and leadership.

To learn more about Langham Partnership and the work we do visit **langham.org**

www.ingramcontent.com/pod-product-compliance
Lightning Source LLC
LaVergne TN
LVHW021619080426
835510LV00019B/2663